How Do You Capture a Monkey?

The Progressive Nature of Sin

Study Guide

Rev. Dr. Tahlib McMicheaux

Table of Contents

Dedication

I dedicate this book to the wonderfully dedicated, mighty men and women of God who selflessly teach the word of God every Sunday and throughout the week. I pray this book, although small yet powerful, becomes a part of your arsenal of weapons geared at creating a defense against enemy forces.

Foreword

It is a humbling task and opportunity to write the Foreword comments to a book that addresses such an important work as Humanity's fall into Sin. In Systematic Theology, the Doctrine of Humanity's fall into sin describes how humans were created good yet succumbed to Satan's temptation to sin. The result is rebellion and falling away from fellowship with God and his original purposes.

In Dr. McMicheaux's book, we seek a clear understanding of sin and how to spot warning signs that lead to the problems of sin. The situation in our American society is that God has been removed from our lives. In 2001, in "Boiling Point," researchers George Barna and Mark Patch concluded that moral anarchy has arrived and dominates our culture today. We now choose which laws of God we believe. The adversary's influence can be resisted and overcome by using the power and tools God has given us. When asked how they form their moral choices, "nearly half of all adults cited their desire to do whatever will bring them the most satisfying results." Only four out of every ten born-again Christians relied on the Bible or church teaching as their primary source of moral guidance," Barna and Hatch "Boiling Point 2001."

This book shows how far society (believers and nonbelievers) has moved from the Bible and Christianity and has accepted living by temporary cultural standards and ethics.

We need to be very clear about how the deceiver works and that he works in stages. He does not just wear a frightening mask and come to you and say, do this or do that. Instead, he insinuates himself into your life gradually, step by step. Recognizing that process and progression is what we will look forward to learning about, not just his tricks, but the corrective actions that we, as Christians, can take to defeat him using the Word of God.

We either have never accepted the Bible as the inerrant word of God, or we have taken a watered-down version that allows us to be in and of the world while never committing to the principles and understanding of who we are.

Introducing the topic of Satan and sin must consider that while the deceiver can insinuate, there needs to be a person susceptible to the influence of the insinuation. The offer is made, but sin cannot take root and flourish without someone accepting and building upon the recommendation (thought).

"Resist the devil, and he will flee." How do we do that? What are the warning signs and how can we respond appropriately?

Dr. Tahlib McMicheaux has opened our vision and understanding of this complex and persistent issue. This book adds an extra dimension for believers and non-believers to explore.

Blessings,

Rev. Dr. Walter J. Clarke

Preface

Being a PK (pastor's kid), the son of Bishop James Curtis McMicheaux, I have heard messages preached about sin all my church-going life, and most of the time it was about how we fall into sin or how sin captures us or how our lust seductively lures us into sin. All being accurate, but absent of the progressive nature of sin. What I have heard over the years has been more or less a two-step process wherein we are tempted, and then we sin. As Pastors, teachers, and educators in these last days, we must share the entire message of the deceitful snares of the enemy. Listen, if the devil is a deceiver of the brethren, there is a strategic and systematic plan contrived and set in motion to capture our souls. This means the enemy is not haphazardly attempting to arrest us but deceptively creating cunning plans to steal us from the Lord. Notice I used the term steal because this implies he is making plans, being strategic, and methodologically plotting his next move, which we must know.

Therefore, my subtopic is the progressive nature of sin. Over the years, I have spent excessive time in prayer and research. From this, I have concluded that there is a deliberate method to the enemies' plot to capture souls. We must sound the alarm. We must have this conversation, teach, and preach about the progressive nature of sin to help believers avoid the enemy's deceptive, cunning, allusive traps.

Having said this let me also say that the overwhelming five progressive steps of sin are a way out. And for this, we should all shout Hallelujah! As I have counseled and coached in several recovery environments, I have heard a cliché repeated from one place to another: When an addicted person decides to, they will stop digging. I do not believe this to be true because if the addicted person holds the shovel, they are tempted to keep digging.

My ideology is that when the addicted person gives up the shovel, the digging stops. The same theory applies to sin, and we must be willing to surrender the shovel. Stop holding on or toying with the thought of letting go or just one more shovel before surrendering. What I am suggesting does not come through the brilliance of our ability to exegesis the word of God, but rather a practical application of the word of God. Many believers are often so lost in their heads that they have forgotten how to use their hearts and souls.

Teachers, preachers, and educators, let's share with the world that we can take back what the enemy has stolen from us by standing firm in the word of God through surrendering, confessing, repenting, and crying out to God. Each level of the progressive nature becomes more challenging, but the hope is that it is still possible for someone to be set free through these four steps to release. I pray God continues to bless your study time in the word of God and that it enhances every sermon, Bible study, and teaching opportunity with truth and wisdom.

Rev. Dr. Tahlib McMicheaux

Introduction

In this book, you will discover how sin develops in a person's heart and how deadly it is. You will also walk away with a better understanding of the progressive nature of sin and addiction. You will understand how temptation becomes an obsession that ultimately leads to death, spiritually and physically.

As you continue to read this book, you will discover that I have extrapolated five words, a part of my subtopics, which create an overall view of our topic through the lens of our subject. Fundamentally, we will explore how lure, temptation, compromise, greed, and obsession outline the progressive nature of sin. In the following chapters, I will detail how to capture a monkey. Progressing through my explanations and examples, you, the reader, will discover that capturing a monkey is like how sin captures the believer. When capturing a monkey, a trap or lure is set in a log that looks like a prize to the betrothed. The prize is nothing more than fool's gold capturing the attention of the one being coerced into a covenant destined for damnation.

All is not lost, however, because one can remove themselves from the holding pattern. It becomes more difficult the longer a person holds onto the prize at the bottom of the log, and the longer one remains in this sinful nature, the harder it is to get out. Satan will trap one's mind to rationalize and justify staying in this sinful situation. The Holy Spirit will nudge you and lead you to the truth of the uneasiness and state of unrest you find yourself in. The feeling of restlessness will not go away. Despite the most genuine arguments, the enemy will supply you with more enticements to keep you in the trap. Here is where I emphasize the solution: choose to obey the commandments of God, resist temptation, repent, and walk in the newness that a life with Christ offers. Is this easy? No, it is not. However, as we traverse the five steps in the progressive nature of sin, unearthing this walk takes discipline, a willingness to see sin for what it is, listening to godly counsel, and having a repentant heart through submitting to the healing grace of God by following the leading of the Holy Spirit.

The story in Matthew 19:16-22 runs through each chapter, weaving a rich, insightful thread in the tapestry that is the progressive nature of sin. As in the story of the rich, young ruler, Jesus offers a person abundant life and freedom, if he follows Him. He provides a lasting alternative to the poison apple that Satan offers. The clincher is that man would choose instant gratification and the lure instead of escaping the jaws of death that are closing in on him. He is unaware that death has set its target on his soul.

Even in today's modern world, we can learn life lessons from this young man who lived in the ancient east. Now I want you to understand that in the progressive process of sin, one can remove themselves at any given time. However, the longer a person remains in this cyclic process, the more difficult it is to get out. Furthermore, I am going to parallel the progressive nature of sin with the progressive nature of addiction to show you that when you find one in a person's life, you will typically find the other.

"For the wages of sin is death, but the gift of God is eternal life in Christ Jesus our Lord" (NKJV, 1975, Romans 6:23).

The way out of the progressive nature of sin can be found in personal revival, which includes conviction, repentance, confession, brokenness, and crying out to God, which creates transformation in one's life. And last, my goal is to give you a mental image of how a primate is captured in the wild and the similarities we as the advanced form of the primate — homosapiens or human beings — are caught and enslaved spiritually.

How Do You Capture a Monkey?

The lion is one of the most feared animals in the jungle. However, the monkey is one of the smartest, most intelligent animals. The lion is revered as the jungle king in Africa, and it is difficult to capture in the wild. Can capturing a monkey be easier? The way to capture a monkey is by hollowing out a log and then making a hole in the log just big enough for the monkey to slip in its open hand. When the monkey walks over to the hollowed-out log and sticks its hand into the hole, grabbing the object at the bottom, its hand will no longer comfortably slide out of the hole. If the monkey holds onto the object at the bottom of the log, it risks hunters finding the pack of monkeys and locating the monkey's whereabouts; the hunters have an easy target, and the monkey is risking death.

Now, here is what happens when the hunter locates the monkey. The monkey senses danger as the hunter approaches and screams in excitement because the monkey's goal is to walk away with the prize at the bottom of the log. The hunter gets closer, and the monkey continues to scream but still will not let go of the object at the bottom of the log. The truth is, all the monkey must do to escape the impending danger is release the object at the bottom of the log. The deciding factor is that this intelligent animal would rather die holding onto the object at the bottom of the log than release it and live.

Why Won't the Monkey Let Go?

Here is why our dear friend won't let go. The monkey will not let go due to lust. Let's see what the Word of God tells us about lust. Sin is revered negatively, but lust is more appealing, like a trifle. But here is the thing; lust is more deadly than sin. Lust is the poisonous viper about to strike. Sin is the state of death you find yourself in afterward, gasping for air as your life force slips away. The lure no longer shines. You have separated yourself from your God and are staring at the dark, bottomless abyss of death. Ghoulish apparitions rise from the deep as a sense of hopelessness engulfs you. What you are experiencing is spiritual death.

Rev. Dr. Tahlib McMicheaux

CHAPTER 1

Lure

Discussion: *Why is it important to know what a lure is, and how do we identify it in our everyday lives?*

[13] "Let no man say when he is tempted, I am tempted of God: for God Cannot be tempted with evil, neither tempteth he any man: [14] but every man is tempted, when he is drawn away of his own lust, and enticed. [15] Then when lust hath conceived, it bringeth forth sin: and sin, when it is finished, bringeth forth death. [16] Do not err, my beloved brethren. [17] Every good gift and every perfect gift is from above and cometh down from the Father of lights, with whom is no variables, neither shadow of turning. [18] Of his own will begat he us with the word of truth, that we should be a kind of first fruits of his creatures." James 1:13-18.

We underestimate the power of lust. This is especially true if we have a form of self-righteousness. Perhaps you attend church regularly, know your Bible, tithe, and consider yourself morally good. The Bible says in 1 Corinthians 10:12 NIV, *"So, if you think you are standing firm, be careful you don't fall!"* The Bible says: If you **think** you are standing firm, guess what? Satan **knows** you better than you know yourself. He has been studying you as he did when he observed Job before attacking him. He knows your weaknesses, your lures. Lust leads to **Lures.** That is why we must go naked before the Father of Light daily. In His Light, we need to be open and honest. We need to look at the so-called passions in our lives. We need to look at the broken parts. Know this, and Satan will attack your wall where it is weakest.

Conceivably, you are in a passionless marriage, whereas he will innocently provide a charismatic, caring shoulder to lean on. Perhaps you are insecure about aging and your looks, and he will offer a gorgeous someone to make you feel so young again. Trust me, my friend, when I say He has many tricks in his shop of horrors. These are subtle lures that your adversary will use, and the lure does not even know that they are the lure. They are also being attacked at their weak point. You are carefully being brought together in the perfect storm. That is how adulterous affairs occur as people fall into the arms of each other, thinking that they are supplying each other's needs. This is a carefully orchestrated trap by the hunter. One can escape this dance of death. It just takes one person to ask, ***"What are we doing?"*** The focus must also be taken from your lure and placed on the weak point in your life. Perhaps it is your marriage. Focus on your marriage. Focus on your spouse. Yes, they may pale compared to your lure at the moment. Satan would have planned it that way. But as you gaze at them through ***the tear-stained eyes of repentance***, the scales of sin fall away, and you will see your spouse or the situation for the beauty that it is. One can release the lure at the bottom of the log and run to the safety of the arms of The Father.

> Romans 8:1-2 says, *"There is no condemnation to them which are in Christ who walk not after the flesh, but after the Spirit."* You would not be condemned if you leave the lure and walk after the Spirit. Verse 2 tells us, *"The law of the Spirit of life in Christ Jesus hath made me free from the law of sin and death."*

Nowadays, no one wants to follow the law. Lines are blurred, and there is no right or wrong way. Do people ask what your philosophy is? What is your worldview? The deadly one is what is your truth? The truth is, the only authentic way that leads to life and away from the perils of temptation is by following the Law of the Holy Spirit through Christ Jesus. Jesus was not controversial when he said, "If your eye causes you to sin, pluck it out." He knew the deadly nature of sin. He was teaching us to have a violent aversion to it. I see it for the fatal viper that it is. He was saying drop it, my child, pluck it out. Run from the lure.

A good friend once told me, "I am trying not to swim into my lure." At that moment, I did not see my friend suffering. In hindsight, I wish I had realized the impending danger of what was happening, and I wish I had been there for my friend. Therein lies the importance of resisting the urge of lust, to deny the desire to swim into the lure. It happens every day in the ocean.

The calm, turquoise waters of the Pacific Ocean appear serene and inviting. A yacht is anchored nearby. A group of men can be seen onboard. They seem to be setting up a rig. The dance of deception is about to begin. They have their eyes on the prize, the proud Blue Marlin. A king of the oceans, with its deadly spines and the ability to effortlessly fly through the air, glides through crystal-clear water at breakneck speeds. How does one lure this behemoth?

Trojan lures mimic the natural movement of the prey this deadly predator hunts. The lure swims and floats just like the delicious squid that the Blue Marlin craves. As the sun shines off the lure, it dances with death.

The Marlin is drawn to the hunt. Heightened predatory instincts override any sense of impending danger. The search is on, but has the hunter become the hunted? On and on, it goes after the lure. Then, in one fell swoop, its jaws clamp onto the deception. Almost immediately, the anglers on the yacht reel in their prize. The Marlin still has a chance to release the lure and escape. There is still time. The circle hook has not yet dug into its cheek. But the proud predator refuses to release its deadly imitation. Like the addictive nature of sin, the longer the Marlin holds on, the deeper the hook entrenches into its flesh until escape is all but impossible. And the fishermen reel it in. To the untrained eye, a Trojan lure, or any lure, appears relatively harmless—pretty and harmless. The stealth of the lure lies in its ability to mimic the movements of what one craves above all else. The promise of untold pleasure. However, it is all mimicry, a seductive, deadly dance.

Consequently, all a lure can ever be is an imitation of the real thing lacking in your life. The high-strung seduction of a passionate temptress will never feel as safe or as comfortable as being in the arms of the wife who has stood with you through the storms of life. So, what drives the person towards the lure? The Blue Marlin can turn around and find an array of delicious fish and squid that will taste far better than the bland mouthful of a rubber lure.

The excitement of the chase is an alluring pleasure that the prize holds; the false sense of need permeates someone and causes them to think they need the lure. Satan would have run you ragged by this time as you chase the lure, late nights chasing, lack of sleep, impaired judgment. You go to sleep thinking of the lure. The first thing you think about upon waking is the lure. It permeates your day. You want to be with the lure; you want to know about the lure. Your identity becomes attached to the lure.

The attraction turns into obsession. All the while, your energy is drained, and you grow weaker and more unsettled. That is the tired state the young man in the story finds himself when he goes to see Jesus. He is run ragged by the chasing of the lure, yet he cannot find the satisfaction he craves, so the story goes.

16 "And, behold one came and said unto him, Good Master, what good thing shall I do, that I may have eternal life? 17 And he said unto him, Why callest thou me good? There is none good but one, that is, God:

But if thou wilt enter into life, keep the commandments. [18] He saith unto him, which? Jesus said, Thou shalt do no murder, Thou shalt not commit adultery, Thou shalt not steal, Thou shalt not bear false witness, [19] Honor thy father and thy mother: and, Thou shalt love thy neighbor as thyself. [20] The young man saith Unto him, all these things have I kept from my youth up: What lack I yet? [21] Jesus said unto him, If thou wilt be perfect, go and sell that thou hast, and give to the poor, and thou shalt have treasure in heaven: and come and follow me. [22] But when the young man heard that saying, he went away sorrowful: for he had great possessions." Matthew 19:16-22.

In the passage above, we see Jesus offering the young man the chance to be perfect, the promise of treasure in heaven, and the invitation to have fellowship with Him. Jesus was a popular teacher of the day; people clamored to be around him. Just getting a personal invitation to join His company should have dawned on the young man that Jesus held him in high esteem, not to mention the promise of treasure in heaven and the chance to be perfect. The young man was a Pharisee, which his sect aimed to achieve by following the law and commandments of Moses. Jesus was offering him perfection by performing one action. *"Go and sell all that thou hast and give to the poor."* Yet this story does not have a happy ending, for the man went away sorrowfully. He held onto his **Lure**, for the Bible says he had great possessions. Having discerned by the Holy Spirit, He saw his hand on the deadly trap. He said, *"Son, let go; sin is at the door of your heart ready to strike a deadly blow."*

Moreover, the first word representing the progressive nature of sin is **Lure.** I suggest that before a person is tempted, they are lured into temptation. The proposition is that the enemy has your lure, and if you are not prayed up, you will take the bait. The enemy is not just plotting how to tempt you but also how to lure you to the temptation.

The noun *Lure* has three (3) meanings:

1. Qualities that attract by seeming to promise some reward (physically, spiritually, or emotionally);

2. Anything that serves as an enticement, and

3. Something used to lure victims into danger.

And here are other words to describe it: **ambush, attraction, bribe, camouflage, carrot, decoy, enticement, fake, gimmick, hook, illusion, inducement, seduction, snare, trap, and trick.**

A lure will attract you by fulfilling a need you did not even know you had. The attraction is like a slow burn at first. The lure is camouflaged as work, yet that is only a decoy that is the enticement of your soul. You may have your life going orderly; although not perfect, your schedule runs like clockwork. You are as happy as anyone else. Then suddenly, you find yourself under ambush. The enemy has been studying the weakness you keep hidden instead of bringing it before God for healing. Satan will start working on creating the so-called perfect, comfortable situation and perhaps staying late at the office, working with a caring colleague.

This fake gimmick creates the illusion of innocence as you spend more time with this person. A friendly touch on the arm and sharing personal problems becomes the bribe that lures you into feeling that you have found a kindred spirit, a covenant friendship to assist you in traversing the choppy waters of life. Yes, Satan can coat a lure in a lot of religious or psychological hogwash to make it palatable against the prick of the Holy Spirit on your conscience, which seems to make you more uncomfortable as the hook digs deeper. "Why does seduction feel so good and so bad?" Because of the opposing forces, to quote John Bunyan in The Pilgrims Progress.

Satan attempts to douse the fire of personal revival in our hearts when we are tempted. Yet behind the wall stands Jesus pouring oil on our fire so the flames burn higher. Even when tempted, Christ does the work by supplying the grace we need to stand firm. In 2 Corinthians 12:9, it says, *"God's grace is enough for us; it is sufficient."* In the worst state of our weakness, when we are enticed, seduced, entrapped, and hooked, His Power will reach down and rescue us. He will wash off the blood caused by the injury of the trap and replace it with the blood of Jesus Christ that speaks a better word. He will cover your nakedness with His robe of righteousness. His righteousness, not yours. That is why Paul says, *"I will boast of my weakness."* This is a man who called himself the worst of sinners. Why this paradox? Paul realized that only when we submit the shortcomings that we keep hidden, a dead marriage, low self-esteem, and our insecurities to Christ, can we release the lure and be saved. This is when the Power of Christ will rest upon us. And oh, what a blessed release to collapse into the arms of the Savior after endlessly and unsuccessfully chasing the lure! But true repentance has to come before one reaches this stage.

Here are some questions to ask yourself when feeling lured to temptation:

1. What is the temptation luring you away from (***Your Savior***)?

2. What is the temptation luring you toward (***Hell***)?

3. Are you being lured into temptation?

"For the wages of sin is death, but the gift of God is eternal life in Christ Jesus our Lord" (New King James Version, 1982 (NKJV), Romans 6:23).

Now, ask yourself these questions: are you being lured into temptation, and are you looking at those weak areas in your life? If you are not, then I can tell you who it is — *your adversary.* Let's look at an example of a lure in the Bible. In the book of Proverbs, lure describes the action of a woman named Folly.

13 "A foolish woman is clamorous; She is simple and knows nothing. 14 For she sits at the door of her house, On a seat by the highest places of the city, 15 To call to those who pass by, Who go straight on their way: 16 Whoever is simple, let him turn in here; And as for him who lacks understanding, she says to him, 17 Stolen water is sweet, And bread eaten in secret is pleasant. 18 But he does not know that the dead are there, That her guests are in the depths of hell." (NKJV, 1982, Proverbs 9:13-18).

I want you to know that every (fish) in the ocean is not lured to temptation. I believe the difference between those who are lured and those who are not are found in this passage.

"But seek first the kingdom of God and His righteousness, and all these things shall be added to you" (NKJV, 1982, Matthew 6:33).

We are easily lured when we give way to the flesh and all its desires. We are easily lured when we give our joy away to the enemy. We are easily lured when we fall into comparison, and everybody else's blessings seem better than our own.

In Matthew 19:16-22, we find the story of the rich young ruler. In this story, we see a young man with his hand caught in a hollowed out log. Wealth is the object placed at the bottom of the log. The hunter who comes to kill this monkey is none other than

Satan. Now I want to tell you that Satan is studying you to find the object to place at the bottom of the log that you will hold on to unto death.

So many believers are so focused on the temptation that they do not even see how they are being lured to it. In this story, if wealth tempted the rich young ruler, what lured him to the temptation? I propose that even before he was tempted, he was lured to temptation, and I believe the same thing happens to us.

The Various Lures

So, the real question is: What lures are you biting at away from the safety of our Lord and Savior Jesus Christ? Here are some big ones: Now, here is the actual death blow because these things are only bad when we place them above the will of God in our lives.

"But seek first the kingdom of God and His righteousness, and all these things shall be added to you" (NKJV, 1982, Matthew 6:33).

The lure grabs your attention to draw you to the temptation. Let's look at the story of the rich young ruler to get more insight into the nature of **Lure.**

The Nature of Lure

[16] *"And, Behold one came and said unto him, Good Master, what good thing shall I do, that I may have eternal life?* [17] *And he said unto him, Why callest thou me good? There is none good but one, that is, God: But if thou wilt enter into life, keep the commandments.* [18] *He saith unto him, which? Jesus said, Thou shalt not commit adultery, Thou shalt not steal, Thou shalt not bear false witness,* [19] *Honor thy father and thy mother: And, Thou shalt love thy neighbor as thyself.* [20] *The young man saith unto him, all these things have I kept from my youth*

up: What lack I yet? ²¹ Jesus said unto him, If thou wilt be perfect, go and sell that thou hast, and give to the poor, and thou shalt have treasure in heaven: and come and follow me. ²² But when the young man heard that saying, he went away sorrowful: for he had great possessions" (NKJV, 1982, Matthew 19:16-22).

When we speak of the sin nature, we refer to the fact that we have a natural inclination to sin; given the choice to do God's will or our own, we will naturally choose to do our own thing, just like the rich young ruler in this story. The sinful nature is that nature in man that makes him rebellious against God. He received wisdom from Jesus, but followed his path to destruction.

Proof that the sinful nature abounds is that no one has to teach a child to lie or to be selfish; instead, we go to great lengths to teach our children to tell the truth and to put others first. Sinful behavior comes naturally. The evening news is filled with tragic examples of humanity misbehaving. Wherever people are, there is trouble.

Charles Spurgeon once said, "As the salt flavors every drop in the Atlantic, so does sin affect every atom of our nature. It is so sadly there, so abundantly there, that if you cannot detect it, you are deceived."

"And it came to pass after these things that his master's wife cast longing eyes on Joseph, and she said, Lie with me" (NKJV, 1982, Genesis 39:7).

How to Bypass a Lure

"Flee also youthful lusts; but pursue righteousness, faith, love, peace with those who call on the Lord out of a pure heart" (NKJV, 1982, 2 Timothy 2:22).

Here is what fish do when the lure hits the water — they run. In the book of Matthew 19:16-22, we find in this story a young man who had his hand caught in a hollowed-out log. Wealth is the object placed at the bottom of the log. The hunter who comes to kill this monkey is none other than Satan.

In this story, was wealth what tempted this rich young ruler? What were his lures? If his bait was wealth, his lure could have been power, clout, status, and want to appear more important than he was. I am going to give you two significant lures that have captured more humans who act like the monkey in this story:

1. *Curiosity*

2. *Insecurity*

Remember, the lure grabs your attention, intending to draw you toward temptation. The lure can be that extra thought, look, flirt, or smile. Lures often catch us off guard when we are in a vulnerable state or when we are susceptible to pride. This is all part of the progressive sin nature.

Protecting Ourselves from the Progressive Nature of Sin

"And do not be conformed to this world, but be transformed by the renewing of your mind, that you may prove what is that good and acceptable and perfect will of God" (NKJV, 1982, Romans 12:22).

"But seek first the kingdom of God and His righteousness, and all these things shall be added to you" (NKJV, 1982, Matthew 6:33).

"For the wages (cost of being steeped in something) of sin is death, but the gift of God is eternal life in Christ Jesus our Lord" (NKJV, 1982, Romans 6:23).

Let's look at what made the rich young ruler compromise his eternal existence for his earthly wealth. Here are two words at the heart of compromising, and the enemy uses them to his advantage.

1. ***Rationalization*** — attempting to explain or justify behavior or an attitude for logical reasons, even if these are inappropriate.

2. ***Justification*** — show or prove to be reasonable.

When you find a person compromising, in most cases, they will have used these two words to justify why they needed the object and why they should hold on to the thing at the bottom of the log.

"When tempted, no one should say, 'God is tempting me.' For God cannot be tempted by evil, nor does He tempt anyone. But each one is tempted when, by his own evil desires he is lured away and enticed. Then After desire has conceived, it gives birth to sin; and sin, when it is full-grown, gives birth to death" (Berean Study Bible, 2016, James 1: 13-15).

Like most of us, when we come to God, we understand what we do not want to give up, like the object at the bottom of the log. Listen, when this young man came to Jesus, he knew what he wanted and did not want to give up. Let's dig into his life for a moment.

1. He was a Jewish leader, which is a significant factor in the story be- cause many of the wealthy Jews of that time were Pharisees, and the Pharisees were the spiritual forefathers of modern-day Judaism.

2. The Pharisees live by the Oral Law. Can this type of person compromise even if they have a firm understanding of the Word of God? Yes.

"Watch and pray so that you will not fall into temptation. The spirit is willing, but the flesh is weak" (NIV, 2011, Matthew 26:41).

Now watch this; what are we watching for? We are watching for lures that will lead us into temptation, causing us to compromise our moral standing with God. Nowadays, we have watered-down versions of the gospel that focuses entirely on self-love and very little on living a disciplined, sinless life. On the other extremity of the scale is a robust Word-based gospel that concentrates solely on avoiding sin. Still, the intended results are impossible to achieve, as they do not believe in the workings of the Holy Spirit in this present age.

The solution to watching for lures in one's life is that you need to be prayed up. You must examine your inner man, take every insecurity, temptation, and doubt before the Father, and lay it down before Him. It would be best if you were honest with your heavenly Father regarding your weaknesses to give no place for the enemy to use your weak points as lures. It would be best to ask the Holy Spirit to help you avoid these lures. He will also give you discernment so that you will see with the spiritual eyes of your understanding.

1. They believed in an afterlife. So, this young man believed in eternal life but felt that something was keeping him from entering eternal life, so he asked Jesus what good things he must do to have what he already believed in.

2. The Pharisees believed God punished the wicked and rewarded the righteous in the world to come.

3. And last, the Pharisees believed in a messiah who would usher in an era of world peace.

The young man was a Pharisee who had compromised his position with God and was now going to the Messiah for help. These Pharisees believed in the word of God, in eternal life, in a reward system that would get him into eternal life, and in a Messiah. Still, because of those two words rationalizing and justifying, he had decided that he wanted eternal life and the banana, which represents the world.

I have one last passage for you:

14 "And unto the angel of the church of the Laodiceans write; These things saith the Lord Amen, the faithful and true witness, the beginning of the creation of God; 15 I know thy works, that thou art neither cold nor hot: I would thou were cold or hot. 16 So then because thou art lukewarm, and neither cold nor hot, I will spew thee out of my mouth. 17 Because thou sayest, I am rich, and increased with goods, and have need of nothing; and knowest not that thou art wretched, and miserable, and poor, and blind, and naked: 18 I counsel thee to buy of me gold tried in the fire, that thou mayest be rich; and white raiment, that thou mayest be clothed, and that the shame of thy nakedness does not appear; and anoint thine eyes with eye salve, that thou mayest see. 19 As many as I love, I rebuke and chasten be zealous, therefore, and repent" Revelation 3:14-19.

God is serious about us not compromising His Word with the world's values. Then some profess to be Christians, yet live lives not holding to the precepts of the Scripture, i.e., compromising their biblical beliefs by living like the world. For them, the things of the world and its sensual allurements take precedence over the Word of God. Jesus referred to these people as *"those who hear the word, but the cares of the world and the deceitfulness of riches and the desires for other things enter and choke the word, and it proves unfruitful."*

"So then, because you are lukewarm, and neither cold nor hot, I will vomit you out of My mouth. Because you say, I am rich, have become wealthy, and have need of nothing—and do not know that you are wretched, miserable, poor, blind, and naked" (NKJV, 1982, Revelation 3:16-17).

These are the ones who, though professing to follow Christ, compromise their faith by craving worldly success at the expense of their moral values. I am sure there is at least one believer who says the next time someone says something, I will give them a piece of my mind and let them know I am a non-compromising person. That is not what I am saying at all. I am saying when you are at work, and your coworkers are swearing like crazy, that is a lure for you if you hear enough. You become an uncompromising person with your life. When that person gets on your last nerve and those choice words cross your mind, remember you are obstinate. When you sit down to watch television and justify and rationalize why it is okay to watch that program versus turning the channel, the program becomes a lure to tempt you into compromising your moral standing with God.

It would be best if you were uncompromising where your feet take you. If you put your hands on something, you need to be uncompromising. You need to be uncompromising with what you listen to. It would be best if you were uncompromising with what you look at. You need to be un- compromising with what you think about, and you need to be uncompromising with the life you live for Christ.

An uncompromising person is a transformed person. The only way you can be altered is through a personal revival. Personal revival allows the operation of the Holy Spirit to have His way in our lives personally vs. collectively. Personal revival is when the prayer is not about our mates but about God changing our hearts first. Personal revival should be the first revival we experience with God.

Today, you might be compromising with the things you are watching on television. You might be compromising with the people you choose to hang out with. You might be compromising with what you choose to allow your mind to think about. You might be compromising with the things you touch with your hands. You might compromise your appearance as a Christian. I want to tell you the Bible reads that God does not like lukewarm believers, and He is about to spew you out like the church in Laodicea. I am asking you to take a stand and become an uncompromising Christian. Not with your words, but with your life. The temptation here is to continue to take the bait or the lure, but with every temptation, there is a way of escape. That way of escape is the Four-Step Release Method. Here are the steps to follow:

1. *Surrender*: The first step in this process is to submit yourself to God and resist the devil wherefore he has to flee from you.

2. *Repentance*: The step of repentance requires you to change your thoughts about the sin you have just come out of. Repentance is more than saying that you won't commit this sin anymore; instead, it is changing how you think about it and believing that it is something God hates. Changing your thoughts will also help you hate what God hates and love what God loves. Your thoughts should comprise pure, lovely, and excellent report.

3. *Confession*: Confessing that we have done something wrong is never easy, but this part of the process is vital because once you confess your sin, the devil no longer has the legal right to hold you hostage to that sin. The saying goes, *we are*

as sick as our secrets, meaning keeping secrets and feelings bottled in will make us sick. Therefore, it is easier to get it out and confess to God that you need His help to overcome your problems.

4. ***Crying out to God***: This fourth and final step takes your heart, mind, and soul wholly involved in freedom and healing. You are lamenting your transgressions to say that you never want to return to such a play where you are out of proper fellowship and communion with your Father. This critical step in the release method gives you clearance and stakes your claim to your liberty. You are in the prime stage to make a speedy turnaround because you are in the first step of the progressive nature of sin. The more you indulge in sin, the more difficult it becomes for you to gain freedom. You discover that bolt of freedom as you continue to the next chapter.

Chapter 1: Lure

Questions to Consider

1. What is the purpose of a *Lure*?

2. How many meanings does the noun *lure* have? What are they?

3. What is temptation luring you away from?

4. What is the temptation luring you to?

5. Why is the power of lust underestimated?

Chapter 1: Lure
Questions to Consider

6. Why did Jesus offer the rich young ruler an invitation to have fellowship with him?

____

____

____

7. What is the first word representing the progressive nature of sin?

____

____

____

8. How does a lure attract you?

____

____

____

9. Why does the enemy study your weakness?

____

____

____

10. Why is it important to confess your sins?

____

____

____

Chapter 1: Lure

Questions to Consider

11. What book of the Bible uses lure as a description for a woman? What is her name?

____

____

____

12. What are the various lures?

____

____

____

13. What is a sinful nature?

____

____

____

14. What were the rich young ruler's lures?

____

____

____

15. What are two powerful lures that have captured more humans who act like the monkey in the story?

____

____

____

Chapter 1: Lure

Questions to Consider

16. How can you protect yourself from the progressive nature of sin?

____

____

____

17. What made the rich young ruler compromise his external existence for earthly wealth?

____

____

____

18. What are the definitions of rationalizing and justifying?

____

____

____

19. What is the only way you can be transformed?

____

____

____

20. What is the Four-Step Release Method?

____

____

____

NOTES

NOTES

CHAPTER 2
Temptation

__Discussion:__ What has caused Christians to believe that God is tempting them, and they merely "fall" into temptation and sin?

16 "And, Behold one came and said unto him, Good Master, what good thing shall I do, that I may have eternal life? 17 And he said unto him, Why callest thou me good? There is non-good but one, God: But if thou wilt enter into life, keep the commandments. 18 He saith unto him, which? Jesus said, Thou shalt not commit adultery, Thou shalt not steal, Thou shalt not bear false witness, 19 Honor thy father and thy mother: and, Thou shalt love thy neighbor as thyself. 20 The young man saith unto him, all these things have I kept from my youth up: What lack I yet? 21 Jesus said unto him, If thou wilt be perfect, go and sell that thou hast, and give to the poor, and thou shalt have treasure in heaven: and come and follow me. 22 But when the young man heard that saying, he went away sorrowful: for he had great possession" (NKJV, 1982, Matthew 19:16-22).

As we climb the ladder of sin's progressive nature, we will succumb to temptation. The goal here is to help you see why this topic is not something God uses to help us learn our lesson. Undoubtedly, it will help you understand the difference between temptation and a trial. You will learn to discern between the one designed by God and the one the enemy designs. At the end of this chapter, you will understand why the rich young ruler walked away sorrowfully and why we, as human beings, hold on to the banana of sin unto death.

Making Worldly Possessions Our God

Now, if the rich, young ruler desired eternal life, what kept him from reaching his desired goal? The only thing Jesus asked of him was for him to sell his worldly possessions and to follow Him. Jesus did not tell him he could never come back to them. He told him to give them up to focus on something more significant than earthly possessions. Jesus knew that the heart of the rich young ruler had gone astray. He knew that this man now placed more value on his possessions than he did in a relationship with Him.

I explained to you how a monkey is caught in the wild. I explained that in Africa, they would take a hollowed-out log with a carved hole just big enough for the monkey to slip its hand inside to reach for the object at the bottom. I relayed our subject topic with the rich young ruler, who desired eternal life but held onto the banana of worldly possessions.

Once the monkey grabs the object at the bottom, its hand will no longer comfortably slide out of the hole. Again, all the monkey needs to do is let go of its desire for worldly possessions.

"But seek first the kingdom of God and His righteousness, and all these things shall be added to you" (NKJV, 1982, Matthew 6:33).

Does God not want us to have worldly possessions? Sure, He does, but He does not want those possessions to become our God.

"For the LORD your God is a consuming fire, a jealous God" (NKJV, 1982, Deuteronomy 4:24).

Jesus knew that the rich young ruler had made his worldly possessions his God, so He told him that if he wanted eternal life, he had to give up his possessions. This was not because they were terrible, but because he had placed them above his desire for the Kingdom of God.

God Does Not Tempt You.

In the previous chapter, we looked at how the monkey identifies the log through the word 'lure', and in this chapter, we want to look at the process that the monkey goes through once it identifies the object at the bottom of the log.

The lure of the monkey is curiosity, and the thing that tempts the monkey is a banana strategically placed at the bottom of the log. Here is another word we use in our Christian language, but I do not believe most truly understand the depth and gravity of this word temptation.

The meaning of this word is (testing designed to strengthen or corrupt). My focus is going to be on the latter of the two. Now, before we move on, let me clear the name of God. God is not tempting you to sin. God has been getting the blame for too long, and it is time to clear it up.

God did not do it. I do not know how often I have heard these words: "I do not understand why God allowed these temptations into my life." I say, "God did not do it."

Somewhere in the life of the rich, young ruler, he was lured. Here is another way to define lure: he gave the lure his attention Temptation overpowered his will. However, if God did not put the object there to tempt him, who did?

[13] *"Let no one say when he is tempted, 'I am tempted by God; for God cannot be tempted by evil, nor does He Himself tempt anyone.* [14] *But each one is tempted when he is drawn away by his own desires and enticed.* [15] *Then, when desire has conceived, it gives birth to sin; and sin, when it is full-grown, brings forth death"* (NKJV, 1982, James 1:13-15).

God's people are people of a disciplined character. Listen, this means when you stop seeking the Kingdom of God in your life and when you stop seeking the will of God in your life, then you will be drawn away and led astray. I understand we all have a curious nature, but did you pray for that before you went after the bait?

An Undisciplined Person

An undisciplined believer is a person who continues to experience God but is never transformed by God. Doubt and lack of faith do not allow them to commit themselves to the process that reaps true transformation. The disciplined believer swims in the same ocean, not biting at the bait or grabbing the banana. When you are undisciplined, you become an easy target for the enemy to lure you to temptation.

"And those who are Christ's have crucified the flesh with its passions and desires" (NKJV, 1982, Galatians 5:24).

We discussed this in the last chapter; curiosity draws us away; insecurity, power, pride, ego, lust, and vain glory distract us. These things lurk in the heart of humanity.

"But each one is tempted when he is drawn away by his own desires and enticed" (NKJV, 1982, James 1:14).

God did not put those temptations in your life. The enemy is spending overtime planting lures all around you; if you are not prayed up, you will bite. At this point is when desire has conceived. The meaning of **conceived**:

- Became pregnant with (a child)

- Formed or devised (a plan or idea) in the mind

Did you know that sin will have you thinking you can outsmart God? I will stick my hand in here, grab this banana, and nobody will ever know. It gives birth to sin and more sin. When it is fully grown, you are in a state of perpetually sinning. When you get to this place, you are holding onto the banana, thinking that no one knows you have progressed from sin to becoming a sinner. You walk around with a banana in your hands as if no one is looking at it.

Here is what sin will do. It will hold you captive. Notice I did not say after you grow up. That is because once you grab onto sin, it has you until it grows up and leads you to death. In our story, the rich, young ruler was lured first and then tempted to grab the banana at the bottom of the log. Temptation touches all your senses and lures or tricks you. The sin at the bottom of the log is a lure. It is used to steer you away from the love of God. In the Australian bush country, there grows a little plant called the "Sundew." It has a slender stem and tiny, round leaves fringed with hairs that glisten with bright drops of liquid as delicate as fine dew. Woe to the insect, however, that dares to dance on it. Although its attractive clusters of red, white, and pink blossoms are harmless, the leaves are deadly. The shiny moisture on each leaf is sticky and will imprison any bug that touches it. As an insect struggles to free itself, the vibration causes the leaves to close tightly around it. This innocent-looking plant then feeds on its victim.

How Do I Fight Temptation?

The question should be: what do I need to do to fight temptation. God cannot be tempted, nor does He tempt anyone, so the temptation is not of God. The Word of God will help you resist the enemy. You have got to put on the whole armor of God. You have got to crucify the old nature daily, and you've got to allow your mind to be transformed.

"We are led astray by our own desires and enticed" (NKJV, 1982, James 1:13-15).

Trials

Now, let's explore the fact that you must *take authority over your life's temptations and praise God for your trials.*

I did not say that our trials would not test us. I did not say that our trials are not uncomfortable. I did not say that you would like your trials, but when you learn the difference between a trial and a temptation, you will praise God for the trials in your life. To glorify God for the trials in your life, you need to know the difference between a trial and a temptation. God does not tempt you, but He will **try** you. Let's define this word.

The word *trial* means:

- Approve or try

- Proof of genuineness

- Trustworthiness

Let me say, some folks are not succeeding in their trials. Some folks are reading this book that is being proven. God is allowing you to go through some trials in your life to prove your genuineness and how trustworthy you are to Him.

"Those who fail to learn from their past are doomed to relive it." — Winston Churchill

When you make Jesus a priority in your life, I believe there is no question whether you can be trusted with Him.

Trusting God

"Behold, I stand at the door and knock. If anyone hears My voice and opens the door, I will come into him and dine with him, and he with Me" (NKJV, 1982, Revelation 3:20).

Why is God so particular about trusting us with the Word? Why does God have to trust us with His Word?

"And was clothed with a vesture dipped in blood: and his name is called The Word of God" (NKJV, 1982, Revelation 19:13).

When you seek God through His Word, He will reveal Himself in His Word. Do you want the power to resist the lures in your life? Get into the word of God daily. Open the door and sup with Jesus.

"Knowing this, that the trying of your faith worketh patience" (NKJV, 1982, James 1:3).

Developing Patience

Let me give you an example of a trial. In the Book of Job, we find a person named Job who was called a righteous man but endured a trial. Job went from riches to poverty. He went from popularity to disdain. His family was taken from him, and his faithful wife abandoned him in his time of need. Job's friends came to console him and later judged and condemned him.

Many of us have read through the Book of Job, only identifying with the experiences but missing the meaning. It becomes clear in this story that Job's trial did not feel good to him. It is also clear that his trials caused him a great deal of discomfort. This book is in the Bible to teach us how to stand in our trials. It tells us when our faith is being tested, stand. When family turns their back on you, stand. Stand when you feel you are carrying the world's weight on your shoulders.

How Do I Know This Was a Trial?

Temptation brings us down, but the trials take us to another level of consciousness. There are four things I have identified about trials:

1. The trial will take you to the edge, but it will not take you over. If you go over, it is probably not a trial. 1 Corinthian 10:3 tells us that God will not put any more on us than we can handle.

2. The trial will test your faith and how committed you are.

3. You will be ministered to in your trial if you are listening.

4. God will get the glory, and you will get the victory from your trial.

"10 And the LORD restored Job's losses when he prayed for his friends. Indeed, the LORD gave Job twice as much as he had before. 11 Then all his brothers, all his sisters, and all those who had been his

acquaintances before came to him and ate food with him in his house, and they consoled him and comforted him for all the adversity that the LORD had brought upon him. Each one gave him a piece of silver and each a ring of gold. ¹² Now the LORD blessed the latter days of Job more than his beginning, for he had fourteen thousand sheep, six thousand camels, one thousand yokes of oxen, and one thousand female donkeys. ¹³ He also had seven sons and three daughters" (NKJV, 1982, Job 42:10-13).

Daniel endured a trial in the lion's den. God got the glory, and Daniel got the victory over his trial. The **three Hebrew boys** endured a trial. God got the glory, and the Hebrew boys got the victory. If you are going through a trial, I need you to mediate on this passage because the enemy wants you to think God has abandoned you.

"No man will be able to stand before you all the days of your life. Just as I have been with Moses, I will be with you; I will not fail you or forsake you" (NASB, 1971, Joshua 1:5).

Just like God brought Job, Daniel, and the three Hebrew boys out victoriously, so will He get you out of your trial with victory!

When Enduring a Trial, Can Satan Slip in a Temptation?

Now, I would be remiss if I did not tell you this. The temptation is there to move you away from your trial so that you will not be proven **genuine and trustworthy**. If Job's situation was considered a trial, what part of his trial was considered a temptation? What part could have led Job to his downfall?

When Job's wife told him to curse God and die when Job's friends told him to admit that the reason he was afflicted physically was because of his sins. When people around him abandoned him, the dogs licked his wounds because there was no one to care for him in his physical state. The lure comes to gain our attention and lead us into temptation. Job's wife was a lure. His friends were lures. His children's deaths became a type of lure. The dogs were a lure. The town's people were lures. The enemy was saying to Job, give me your attention, but Job, who was committed in his walk, said, **"To God be the glory"** (I am paraphrasing). When Job's wife told him to curse God and die, Job lifted his head and said, *"The Lord giveth, and the Lord taketh, blessed be the name of the Lord."*

Despite my situation, Job said, **"To God be the glory."** Lord, I am in the throes of my trial, and it does not feel good, but **"To God be the glory."** I am being tested on all sides, but **"To God be the glory.** My friends have abandoned me, but **"To God be the glory."** The doctors say they cannot see how I am going to make it out, but **"To God be the glory."**

I am going to leave you with four pointers about trials:

1. God will not leave me or forsake me.

2. Your trials will not last forever.

3. Your trials are an opportunity to show God that you are genuine and trustworthy.

4. When God brings me out, He will get the glory for my victory.

We All Face Temptation.

The Scriptures tell us we all face temptations. 1 Corinthians 10:13 says, *"No temptation has overtaken you, but such as is common to man."*

Perhaps this provides a little encouragement, as we often feel the world is bearing in on us alone and that others are immune to temptations. We are told that Christ was also tempted.

"For we do not have a high priest who cannot sympathize with our weaknesses, but One who has been tempted in all things as we are, yet without sin" (NKJV, 1982, Hebrews 4:15).

From where do these temptations come? First, they do not come from God, although He allows them. James 1:13 says, *"For God cannot be tempted by evil, and He does not tempt anyone."*

In the first chapter of Job, we see God allowed Satan to tempt Job, but with restrictions. Satan is roaming on the earth like a lion, seeking people to devour (1 Peter 5:8). Verse 9 tells us to resist him, knowing that other Christians are also experiencing his attacks.

By these passages, we can know that temptations come from Satan. James 1:14 shows the temptation in us as well. We are tempted when *"carried away and enticed by our own lust."*

We allow ourselves to think specific thoughts, go places we should not, and make decisions based on the lusts that lead us into temptation.

Resisting Temptation

How do we resist temptations? First, we must return to the example of Jesus being tempted in the wilderness by Satan in Matthew 4:1-11. Each of Satan's temptations was met with the same answer: *"It is written,"* followed by scripture. If the Son of God used the Word of God to effectively end the temptations, which we know works because after three failed efforts, *"the devil left him"* (v. 11), how much more do we need to use it to resist our temptations?

All our efforts to resist will be ineffective unless they are powered by the Holy Spirit through constant reading, studying, and meditating on the Word. In this way, we will be *"transformed by the renewing of your mind"* Romans 12:2. There is no other weapon against temptation except the *"Sword of the Spirit,"* which is the Word of God in Ephesians 6:17.

Colossians 3:2 says, *"Set your mind on the things above, not on the things on earth."* If our minds are filled with the latest TV shows, music, and all the rest that the culture offers, we will be bombarded with messages and images that inevitably lead to sinful lusts. But if our minds are filled with the majesty and holiness of God, the love and compassion of Christ, and the brilliance of both reflected in His perfect Word, we find that our interest in the lusts of the world diminishes and disappears. But without the Word's influence on our minds, we are open to anything Satan wants to throw at us.

Guarding Our Hearts

Here, then, is the only means to guard our hearts and minds to keep the sources of temptation away from us. Remember the words of Christ to His disciples in the garden on the night of His betrayal:

"Keep watching and praying that you may not enter into temptation; the spirit is willing, but the flesh is weak" (NKJV, 1982, Matthew 26:41).

Most Christians would not openly want to jump into sin, yet we cannot resist it because our flesh is not strong enough to resist. We place ourselves in situations or fill our minds with lustful passions, leading to sin. One of the synonyms to describe lure is to entice. Entice means to attract or tempt by offering pleasure or advantage. We are drawn through our imagination, desires, physical pleasure, spiritual power, and emotional dominance. In other words, the lures of enticement are all around us.

Conceiving Sin

People are tempted when they are drawn away by their desires, and the desires become enticing. To be tempted, you need to tap into a passion already there. Let's talk about conceiving to understand what James is honestly saying. Do you know that sinful nature is already there when you are born? When you accept Jesus, you are washed by the lamb's blood. From this point, each of us must crucify the old nature daily. To conceive a human being, it takes the egg and the sperm cell. Both are already there in the person lying dormant until it contacts one another.

We also understand that positive thought is birth in the same way, but sinful nature is like mixing oil and water. They do not cohabitate. When you cannot crucify your sinful nature and desire meets with that, it gives birth to something that now takes on its existence within our sphere. Once the sinful nature is born in man based on negative desire, it is conceived into full-blown pregnancy. In the pregnancy stage of sin, a person is led, controlled, and dominated unto submission by the conceived sin until that sin ultimately leads the person to death.

"For the wages of sin is death, but the gift of God is eternal life in Christ Jesus our Lord" (NKJV, 1982, Romans 6:23).

From the book of James, we understand that sin has its nature and can be conceived in a person's life, and that person can struggle with sin throughout the pregnancy, just like a mother struggles with giving birth to a baby. However, the goal of sinful nature is not to bring forth life but to bring forth death spiritually, mentally, or physically.

The Progressive Nature of Addiction vs. Sin

"Do you not know that to whom you present yourselves slaves to obey, you are that one's slaves whom you obey, whether of sin leading to death, or of obedience leading to righteousness" (NKJV, 1982, Romans 6:16)?

"No temptation has overtaken you except such as is common to man, but God is faithful, who will not allow you to be tempted beyond what you are able, but with the temptation will also make the way of escape, that you may be able to bear it" (NKJV, 1982, 1 Corinthians 10:13).

We have looked at some verses that referenced addiction, and most alluded to the addict. I want to show you that when Jesus went to the cross, your addiction and behaviors that are not edifying to God were nailed to the cross with Him, and when He came down, He left them hanging up there. When you succumb to your addiction, do not blame it on God because He sent His son to die on the cross. The truth about these two words is that there isn't much difference. We make excuses for ourselves in the church because we are not dealing with substance abuse. That's not the only addiction there is. People have a habit of attitude, behavior, and excuses. This book is essential because when we are honest with ourselves and Christ, we can seek healing from God. So, let us define these two words.

Addiction

An addict is a person addicted to a particular substance, typically an illegal drug. However, an addict can be considered an enthusiastic devotee of a specified thing or activity.

Addiction: this is the fact or condition of being addicted to a substance, thing, or activity.

So anybody can be addicted, and there is not much difference between addiction and the addict. Now, I am sure someone is asking him- or herself: *Why are you spending so much time on addiction?"* Here is why. Addictions are nothing more than repeated behaviors we make excuses for and succumb to. So, if we look at how addictions are formed through behaviors, we can decide to change the behavior. Addictions are consistent and repeated behaviors that do not edify God's kingdom. So, let's ask: *Do you have some repeated and consistent behaviors that are not edifying the Kingdom of God?*

Addictive Behaviors

"Do you not know that you are the temple of God and that the Spirit of God dwells in you? If anyone defiles the temple of God, God will destroy him. For the temple of God is holy, which temple you are" (NKJV, 1982, 1 Corinthians 3: 16-17).

Does lying destroy the temple? Does gossiping destroy the temple? Does backbiting destroy the temple? Does excessively eating destroy the temple? Does eating the wrong foods destroy the temple? Do drugs destroy the temple? Does alcohol destroy the temple? If all these things can destroy the temple and are addictive, we have some addicts in the church who need prayer. We need to stop pretending it is just a little sin problem. It is an addiction problem. Like the key to personal revival is owning your baggage, the key to addictions is being honest with yourself.

Getting beyond addiction requires being honest with God. Here is the deal. How can you be honest with God when you are not honest with yourself? So, what we are talking about is human behavior. Now all of us are subject to human behavior. However, the real deal comes in when we stop attempting to crucify the flesh, spirit, and mind daily and begin excusing away our behaviors.

When these behaviors manifest themselves repetitively, and we continue to make excuses for them, they become addictions. Here is another reason I am belaboring addictions: when you succumb to these addictive behaviors, you lower the standard that God has called you to live by. Now here is what happens when your ideals are reduced. You open the door for the enemy to come in through these five points.

The Five Points of Addictive Behavior

Trigger: *an act or event that serves as a stimulus and starts or precipitates a reaction or series of responses.*

If I wrote this right, the addictive behavior would mean anything like eating ice cream and candy. Let's not stop there because I know some believers are triggered by a few words that cause them to lay their Bibles down. The point of all this is for you to look at some of your responses to the triggers in your life. Are you giving in to the triggers, or are you resisting those triggers? I looked at some of my triggers. Arrogant and lazy people set me off. Now here is the real deal. Those people I am triggered by do not have anything to do with my triggers. When I am prayed up and have surrendered my triggers to God, those people do not bother me as much. If you are being triggered, maybe you need to ask yourself, are you prayed up?

Surrender: *cease resistance to an enemy and submit to their authority.*

When I am triggered and surrender to the trigger, I give my power away to hostile forces that want nothing more than to lead me away from God's will. The moment I cease resisting the enemy implies a lack of being prayed up in the Spirit. The candy bar does not have power over me when I am prayed up. When I am prayed up, the ice cream does not have authority over me; when I am prayed up, the argument does not have power over me.

"Yet in all these things, we are more than conquerors through Him who loved us" (NKJV, 1982, Romans 8:3).

What behavior has become a part of your DNA and is not edifying the Kingdom of God?

Value: *relative worth, merit, or importance; estimated or assigned worth:*

Now, here is what we do. We give these negative behaviors value in our lives, and over a period, through making excuses, they become addictions or compulsive behaviors. These negative behaviors are given worth, merit, and importance in our lives as we rationalize and justify their existence. What consistent negative behavior have you given value to in your life? A behavior that is so consistent it could be called an addiction.

Craving: *an extreme desire for something.*

Now, here is what happens when we give these negative behaviors worth. Our spirit craves these things that are not edifying to the Kingdom of God. You might wonder why gossip and drama seem to find specific people. It's because they are craving it in their spirit. People seek these things out in their lives when they have these cravings. Here is the reality about these people: "Their minds have not been renewed." That old nature is still craving the old ways of the world. We have a lot of believers who have dressed up the outside, but inwardly they are still wrestling with the ancient nature of the world. When your mind has been transformed, you lose those old ways, behaviors, desires, attitudes, cravings, and dispositions.

"And do not be conformed to this world, but be transformed by the renewing of your mind, that you may prove what is that good and acceptable and perfect will of God" (NKJV, 1982, Romans 12:2).

The Bible reads God cannot abide in an unclean temple, so if your spirit is craving negative behavior, guess who is not in your temple.

Identity: *who someone is, the name of a person, the qualities, beliefs, etc., that make a particular person or group different from others.*

People define themselves by their addiction and justify it, while their behavior affects the world around them. You know how we say, "That is just who I am. That is just what I do. You know how I was when you married me!"

This writing on addiction allows believers to examine their behavior and pray to God about their justified ways and excuses. The ways you know are robbing you of being a believer. Those ways that are defiling the temple, those ways that are affecting the surrounding people. Those ways have caused you to lay down your Bible, your beliefs, and even your Savior. Such practices are not suitable for the Kingdom of God. Once you have evaluated your ways, you are one step closer to gaining freedom through the Four-Step Release Method that follows:

1. Surrender
2. Repentance
3. Confession
4. Crying out to God

Whether you are entangled in a turbulent situation or dabbling in an addiction that has a hold on you, there is hope! The progressive nature of sin can trap you at any stage, and the Four-Step release method is your way out. Each chapter will mention these steps because they are essential to your renewal and personal revival.

"Repent therefore and be converted, that your sins may be blotted out, so that times of refreshing may come from the presence of the Lord" (NKJV, 1982, Acts 3:19).

Chapter 2: Temptation
Questions to Consider

1. What kept the rich, young ruler from reaching his desired goal?

    ____

    ____

    ____

2. What is the definition of the word temptation?

    ____

    ____

    ____

3. What type of person continues to experience God but is never transformed by God?

    ____

    ____

    ____

4. What stops a person from being transformed by God?

    ____

    ____

    ____

5. What makes you an easy target for the enemy?

    ____

    ____

    ____

Chapter 2: Temptation
Questions to Consider

6. How do I fight temptation?

____

____

____

7. When have you progressed from sinning to being a sinner?

____

____

____

8. Is God tempting me?

____

____

____

9. How do I praise God for trials in my life when I am going through them?

____

____

____

10. Why is God so particular about trusting us with the Word? Why does God have to trust us with His Word?

____

____

____

Chapter 2: Temptation
Questions to Consider

45

11. What is an example of a trial?

12. What is the purpose of temptation and trials?

13. What will a trial do in your life?

14. What is the guaranteed outcome of going through a trial?

15. When enduring a trial, can Satan bring temptation into my life?

Chapter 2: Temptation
Questions to Consider

16. What do we know about trials?

____

____

____

17. From where do these temptations come?

____

____

____

18. How do we resist temptations?

____

____

____

19. How are we drawn into sin?

____

____

____

20. What are addictions?

____

____

____

NOTES

NOTES

CHAPTER 3
Compromise

Discussion: *What is compromise's significant role in the enemy's plan against your life?*

Concluding chapter two with the addictive behavior of believers ushers us into the world of compromise. When one is addicted to a particular thing or a way of being, they can often be blinded to the gods they have bowed, thus compromising their walk with a Holy God and inevitably becoming more ensnared to sin. Over the last few chapters, we have learned that the progressive sin nature begins with being lured by the enemy to temptation. Once you have been tempted, it becomes the enemy's goal to get you into a compromising position. Let's look at this word's power in the Christian vernacular. This is a very understated word, but the impact of this word devastates the lives of people in the Christian community. I want to show you that life and death for the believers hang on to this word. This word wreaks havoc on the Christian community and is as lethal as gas leaking in a closed building because the outcome is equally explosive.

Defining Compromise

Compromise: *a settlement of differences in which each side makes a concession.*

Well, that does not sound so bad. However, I do not want to concede with the enemy; every time I compromise, that is what I am doing. I am compromising my moral standards.

1.   *Something that combines qualities or elements of different things*

This is kind of like trying to put oil and water together.

"I hate double-minded people, but I love your law" (NIV, 2011, *Psalm 119:113).*

So, compromising is a little of this and a bit of that or a person wanting to stand on both sides of the road.

2.   *A weakening or reduction of one's principles or standards*

Now we get to the heart of the purpose of forcing us into compromising positions in our lives. Every time we compromise, our spiritual immune system is weakened.

3.   *Impairment*

Did you know that compromising weakens moral judgment and impairs spiritual stamina? What does impair mean? It means *weaken.*

When someone tells you your immune system is compromised, they say it has been weakened. This means that a hostile force has infiltrated your system, and it has now rendered your system helpless to defend itself. It means your system is infected with something foreign that is warring against that which is good. It means your system has been broken down into a state of vulnerability. Your system is now compromised.

Compromising People

The enemy has weakened many believers through this word, and the church has become a breeding ground for people who want to stand on both sides of the fence. People are walking around with compromised immune systems. Now you want to know why compromising believers prefer to be around compromising people. Because uncompromising people will hold them accountable for living up to a higher standard, let's look at what the Bible says about compromising people.

"No one can serve two masters. Either you will hate the one and love the other, or you will be devoted to the one and despise the other. You cannot serve both God and money." (NIV, 2011, Matthew 6:24).

A compromising person wants the best of both worlds. For those of you who are secretly or even openly compromising your moral standards, I want to tell you that this will cost you your salvation. Stop today and become an uncompromising believer.

You Cannot Fool God.

What if I told you God would allow you to go through life thinking that you have fooled everyone around you, only to discover that you did not deceive Him?

"Not everyone who says to me, 'Lord, Lord,' will enter the kingdom of heaven, but only the one who does the will of my Father who is in heaven. Many will say to me on that day, 'Lord, Lord, did we not prophesy in your name and your name drive out demons and, in your name, perform many miracles?' Then I will tell them plainly, 'I never knew you. Away from me you evildoers" (NIV, 2011, Matthew 7:21-23)!

A Double-Minded Person

"A double-minded man is unstable in all his ways" James 1:8.

Do you want to know what God thinks about your decision to compromise with the enemy? You are unstable in all your ways, so even when you come to church and get your hallelujahs on, God is saying you are only double-minded. God is saying you are unstable in your home, on your job, at the supermarket in all your ways, and wherever you take yourself. I propose to you that the actual damage in the progressive sin nature begins here, for it is here that you are shifted away from your moral standing as a believer.

Compromising is the first phase of the internal demise of our will to resist the enemy. For the moment you compromise, you have given the enemy power over your life. Each compromise weakens your spiritual immune system until it leads you to spiritual death. I will provide a passionate plea to everyone who realizes they are now in a compromising position. Maybe you are compromising with what you watch; what you listen to, the people you are hanging out with; the things you choose to think about. Listen, the enemy wants to weaken your spiritual immune system.

Getting to Know the Rich Young Ruler

[16] "And, Behold one came and said unto him, Good Master, what good thing shall I do, that I may have eternal life? [17] And he said unto him, why callest thou me good? There is non-good but one, God: But if thou wilt enter life, keep the commandments. [18] He saith unto him, which? Jesus said Thou shalt not commit adultery, Thou shalt not steal, Thou shalt not bear false witness, [19] Honor thy father and thy mother: and, Thou shalt love thy neighbor as thyself. [20] The young man saith unto him, all these things have I kept from my youth up: What lack I yet? [21]

Jesus said unto him, If thou wilt be perfect, go and sell that thou hast, and give to the poor, and thou shalt have treasure in heaven: and come and follow me. 22 But when the young man heard that saying, he went away sorrowful: for he had great possessions" (NKJV, 1982, Matthew 19:16-22).

We will spend some time getting to know this person who calls himself the **Rich Young Ruler**. And look at why he will compromise his eternal existence for wealth. However, before I move on, I will give you two words at the heart and core of compromising, and the enemy uses them both to his advantage.

1. Rationalizing

2. Justifying

When you find a compromising person, you will most likely find someone astute at rationalizing and justifying things to work out in their favor. In most cases, this person has used two words to explain why they needed the object at the bottom of the log. They rationalize they need to hold on to the thing, just like the illustration of the monkey who refused to let go of the banana.

Matthew 19:16 reads, *"And, Behold, one came and said unto him, Good Master, what good thing shall I do, that I may have eternal life?"*

Here is what he is saying. I know there are Ten Commandments, but give me one to keep justifying breaking the other nine. I want you to see in this passage the process had already begun before the rich young ruler approached Jesus. He had already been lured; he had already been tempted, and he had already compromised his moral principles. His rationalizing and justifying made him conclude that if he could keep one commandment, then maybe that would be good enough to get him into heaven. When this young man came to Jesus, he knew what he wanted and did not want to give up. Like most of us, when we come to God with one hand holding onto the banana.

The Life of the Rich Young Ruler

First, I want to point out this rich young ruler was a Jewish leader. The Greek word for "ruler" in this context refers to a "leader" or an "official" of some sort. They would have had administrative authority. This story is a significant development because if he was a Jewish official and a wealthy Jewish official, he was probably a part of the Pharisees group, perhaps a leader in the local synagogue, or even a member of the Sanhedrin. The Pharisees were a group that could be defined as the religious elitist and separatist of their time. Most Pharisees were wealthy and thought themselves too good or too holy to relate to the common folk. The Pharisees were the spiritual forefathers of modern-day Judaism.

The Pharisees lived by the Oral Law. They believed that the Law God gave Moses was twofold: the Written Law and the Oral Law, i.e., the prophets' teachings and the Jewish people's oral traditions. The commandments were a part of the law that the Pharisees lived by. Can a person compromise even if they have a firm understanding of the Word of God? Yes. All it takes is for that person to give attention to the lure in their lives, leading to temptation and compromise.

The Pharisees also believed in an afterlife. This young man believed in eternal life but felt that something was missing in his spiritual life because he asked Jesus, "What good thing must I do to have eternal life?" This is clear. As the text shows, he believes he has been scrupulously faithful in keeping all the commandments, but he senses that this alone cannot be enough.

The Pharisees believed God punished the wicked and rewarded the righteous in the world to come. He believed that gaining the reward of eternal life depended on doing great works rather than salvation being something that requires child-like faith. *And last, the Pharisees believed in a Messiah who would usher in an era of world peace.* Let's look at everything I just wrote. This rich young ruler believed in the Word given to Moses and the commandments. Even if he did not keep them, he believed in eternal life. He believed in the Messiah. He believed in paying the price for not following God's Word. Why didn't he give up his wealth for eternal life if he believed in all this? Somewhere in his life, he had been lured to temptation and grabbed onto the world's desires while being tempted. His mind became filled with justifying and rationalizing why he should hold on to the banana in his hand, even if it cost him his eternal life.

The Uncompromising Believer

The last passage in this chapter sums it all up:

*14 "And unto the angel of the church of the Laodiceans write; These things saith the Lord Amen, the faithful and true witness, the beginning of the creation of God; 15 I know thy works, that thou art neither cold nor hot: I would thou were cold or hot. 16 So then, because thou art lukewarm and neither cold nor hot, I will spew thee out of my mouth. 17 Because thou sayest, I am rich, and increased with goods, and have need of nothing; and knowest not that thou art wretched, and miserable, and poor, and blind, and naked. 18 I counsel thee to buy of me gold tried in the fire, that thou mayest be rich; and white raiment, that thou mayest be clothed, and that the shame of thy nakedness does not appear; and anoint thine eyes with eye salve, that thou mayest see. 19 As many as I love, I rebuke and chasten: be zealous, therefore, and repent."
Revelation 3: 14-19*

God is serious about us not compromising His Word with the values of this world. Some profess to be Christians, yet live lives that are not in keeping with the precepts of the scripture, i.e., compromising their biblical beliefs by living like the world. For them, the things of the world and its sensual allurements take precedence over the Word of God. Jesus referred to these people as:

"Those who hear the word, but the care of the world and the deceitfulness of riches and the desires for other things, enter in and choke the word, and it proves unfruitful" (NKJV, 1982, Matthew 13:22).

Someone might read this saying, "I have the license to give the world a piece of my mind because I need to let them know I am an uncompromising believer." These individuals are the ones who, though professing to follow Christ, compromise their faith by craving worldly success and accolades from their fellow man. This is the call to being an uncompromising believer.

That is not what I am saying at all. I am saying that when you are at work, and your co-workers are cursing like sailors, you become an uncompromising believer in your life. When you sit down to watch television and justify and rationalize why watching that program is okay, you need to remind yourself that you are an uncompromising believer. When that person gets on your last nerve and those choice words cross your mind, remember, you are an adamant, transformed believer. It is important to be uncompromising with where your feet go. You need to be uncompromising with what you put your hands on. You need to be uncompromising with what you listen to. You need to be uncompromising with what you look at. You need to be uncompromising with what you think about, and you need to be uncompromising with the life you live for Christ.

An uncompromising person is a transformed person. The only way you can be changed is through a personal revival. Today, you might compromise with what you are watching on television. You might compromise with the people you choose to hang out with.

You might compromise with what you decide to allow your mind to think about. You might compromise with the things that you touch with your hands. You might compromise your appearance as a Christian.

I want to tell you the Bible says that God does not like lukewarm believers, and He is about to spew you out like the church in Laodicea. Today, I am asking you to stand and become an uncompromising Christian — not with your words, but with your life. You may wonder how one does that. Although the process is not simple, the solution is found in the Four-Step Release Method: Surrender, Repentance, Confession, and Crying out to God.

Compromising your walk with God not only hinders you, but it confuses others that are seeking to follow Christ as well. God is not the author of such confusion, and confusion is a way for the enemy of your soul to get a foothold in your life. Praying a prayer of surrender to God will put you back on the right track. With surrender comes repentance, which is changing your mind about the thing you are compromising on. As you repent, you confess that you have compromised and allowed the enemy to have legal rights in your life. Confession then opens the way for you to cry out to God. He hears you; because of His grace and mercy, we are not consumed.

Chapter 3: Compromise

Questions to Consider

1. What is compromise?

   ____

   ____

   ____

2. Why do compromising believers prefer to be around compromising people?

   ____

   ____

   ____

3. Why would God allow you to go through life thinking you have fooled everyone around you, only to discover you have not deceived Him?

   ____

   ____

   ____

4. Do you want to know what God thinks about your decision to compromise with the enemy?

   ____

   ____

   ____

5. What is the first phase of the internal demise of our will to resist the enemy?

   ____

   ____

   ____

Chapter 3: Compromise
Questions to Consider

6. Who lived by the Oral Law?

7. How can the adversary's influence be resisted and overcome?

8. How do we resist the devil?

9. What are the warning signs, and how can we respond appropriately?

10. Why didn't the Rich Young Ruler give up his wealth for eternal life if he believed in eternal life, the Ten Commandments, and the Messiah?

Chapter 3: Compromise
Questions to Consider

11. What is a way that you can be transformed?

____

____

____

12. When you find a compromising person, you will most likely find what?

____

____

____

13. Who was the rich young ruler?

____

____

____

14. What did the Pharisees believe?

____

____

____

15. Can a person compromise even if they have a firm understanding of the Word of God?

____

____

____

Chapter 3: Compromise
Questions to Consider

16. Why do some progressing Christians live lives that are not keeping with the precepts of the scripture?

____

____

____

17. What does Jesus refer to these people as?

____

____

____

18. What makes a person an uncompromising believer?

____

____

____

19. What does compromising your walk with God do to your spiritual life?

____

____

____

20. What is the Four-Step Release Method?

____

____

____

NOTES

NOTES

CHAPTER 4
Greed

<u>*Discussion:*</u> *How does a believer get entangled in the web of greed?*

Greed and the Sin Nature

"And, Behold one came and said unto him, Good Master, what good thing shall I do, that I may have eternal life?" And he said unto him, Why callest thou me good? There is non-good but one, God: But if thou wilt enter life, keep the commandments. He saith unto him, which? Jesus said Thou shalt not commit adultery, Thou shalt not steal, Thou shalt not bear false witness, Honor thy father and thy mother: and, Thou shalt love thy neighbor as thyself. The young man saith unto him, all these things have I kept from my youth up: What lack I yet? Jesus said unto him, "If thou wilt be perfect, go and sell that thou hast, and give to the poor, and thou shalt have treasure in heaven: and come and follow me." But when the young man heard that saying, he went away sorrowful: for he had great possession (NKJV, 1982, Matthew 19:16-22).

As we move up the progressive nature of sin, our next word is **greed.** Did you know people can become greedy in their sinful nature? Did you know that once a person compromises and enters rationalizing and justifying, greed becomes an overpowering behavior that causes a person to think, act, and behave unreasonably? Changing this behavior from this point on becomes challenging. So, let's define the word *greed*. *Greed* is an overwhelming urge to have *more* of something, usually more than what you need. Every reader has been guilty of being greedy at some point. I want you to think about where greed has crept into your life, and then I want you to ask yourself, "What am I going to do about it? I am not just going to write about greed; I want you to see greed in action. Greed is a desire to have more than you need. Greed comes from money, clothes, television, food, drinking, or anything else we do in excess. If a little is good, a lot is better.

The Spirit of Greed

Have you ever watched little kids at a birthday party furiously grabbing candy that has fallen on the ground from a piñata? It is rare to find a child that will stop and say to their parents, "I've got enough." From where did this spirit come? Satan's jealousy in heaven turned into greed because he could not get enough power. The power he was given in heaven was not enough for him, so he started looking and desiring to have the power of God. Jealousy and greed got Satan kicked out of heaven. I question, "Where is greed about to take you into your life?" So, the spirit of greed is the same one that got kicked out of heaven. It is now running rampant throughout the earth. When you see greed, it is an ugly spirit that causes the soul of humankind to become contorted, seeking only to please self. The spirit of greed can take and never return. The spirit of greed can hurt, and never look back at the pain it is caused. No age limits, no sexual preference, and no cultural barriers make up the sickness of greed. Greed transcends race, gender, and education. Greed also transcends religion.

Let me show you two scriptures that tell us why God hates greed:

"The second is this, `You shall love your neighbor as yourself.' There is no other commandment greater than these" (RSV, 1952, Mark 12:31).

"Therefore, whatever you want men to do to you, do also to them, for this is the Law and the Prophets" (NKJV, 1982, Matthew 7:12).

God hates greed because it is devoid of empathy and compassion.

The Ugly Nature of Greed

We are going to look at greed through the life of a well-known biblical character by the name of King David. He is going to show us the ugliness of greed. David will show us what we do not want to see when we are in the throes of greed. I want to show you greed, up close and personal.

[1] *"It happened in the spring of the year, at the time when kings go out to battle, that David sent Joab and his servants with him, and all Israel, and they destroyed the people of Ammon and besieged Rabbah. But David remained in Jerusalem."*

[2] *"Then it happened one evening that David arose from his bed and walked on the roof of the king's house. And from the roof, he saw a woman bathing, and the woman was very beautiful to behold."*

[3] *"So, David sent and inquired about the woman. And someone said, "Is this not Bathsheba, the daughter of Eliam, the wife of Uriah the Hittite?"*

[4] *"Then David sent messengers and took her, and she came to him, and he lay with her, for she was cleansed from her impurity; and she returned to her house."*

[5] *"And the woman conceived, so she sent and told David and said, "I am with child."*

[6] *"Then David sent to Joab, saying, '"Send me Uriah the Hittite."' And Joab sent Uriah to David."*

[7] *"When Uriah had come to him, David asked how Joab was doing, how the people were doing, and how the war prospered."*

[8] *"And David said to Uriah, '"Go down to your house and wash your feet."' So Uriah departed from the king's house, and a gift of food from the king followed him."*

[9] *"But Uriah slept at the door of the king's house with all the servants of his lord and did not go down to his house." (NKJV, 1982, 2 Samuel 11:1-9).*

Vs. 1. David moves out of the will of the Lord;
Vs. 2. David sees the lure;
Vs. 3. David responds to the lure with temptation;
Vs. 4. David compromises his moral standing with God;

Vs. 5. David justifies, rationalizes, and attempts to cover up his sins. David had fallen out of personal revival by operating in unadulterated evil. The first step in personal revival is to own your sins before God;

Vs. 15. David has Uriah killed to cover up his sin, and now he gets to have Bathsheba any time he wants.

So far in this story, we have looked at David

- Being out of the will of God;

- Grabbing onto the lures in his life;

- Being tempted;

- Compromising his moral standing with God;

- And desiring someone else's position.

The Pitfalls of Rationalizing and Justifying

We will focus on reading 2 Samuel, Chapter 12:1-7 since it took the prophet Nathan to show David the greed in his heart. People can become selfishly blinded by desire in their lives.

The monkey rationalizes and justifies why he should hold on to the banana. The longer the monkey holds onto the banana, the stronger the desire to explain and justify it gets until it surfaces in the raw, aggressive nature called greed. Greed tells the monkey this is his banana and even rationalizes why holding onto the banana is necessary, even with the threat of death. Greed will twist the mind, blind the heart, and weaken the soul. In believers, greed is a silent killer.

"The greedy bring ruin to their households, but the one who hates bribes will live" (NIV, 2011, Proverbs 15:27).

The definition of **greed** from the Bible Dictionary: *n. 1. Greed is the defining characteristic of human nature. 2. The desire to own or control more resources than others. Greed is not merely "I want more." Greed is "I want more than everybody else."*

The outcome of our greed does not just impact our lives; it affects every life around us.

"Woe to him who builds his house by unjust gain, setting his nest on high to escape the clutches of ruin! You have plotted the ruin of many peoples, shaming your own house and forfeiting your life" (NIV, 2011, Habakkuk 2:9-10).

Money and Greed

Money and greed are discussed throughout the entire Bible. In fact, Jesus talked about this issue more than any other, except for the Kingdom of God. As humans, we start life as newborns in a state of rebellion. We are born into sin, and that remains until we enter personal revival, allowing our lives to be transformed by the blood of Jesus Christ.

This statement is straightforward. Greed cannot be a part of your life if you are a believer. Heaven will not receive you if you practice greed daily. When you live in a compulsive, obsessive state and think the world is all about you, your greed has overtaken your will to resist.

The Lifestyle of Greed

"They are darkened in their understanding and separated from the life of God because of the ignorance that is in them due to the hardening of their hearts" (NIV, 2011, Ephesians 4:18).

Greed not only blinds you, but it hardens your heart, causing you to hold onto the banana, as you justify why you can't let go. *Greed* comes from the Old English *grædig* or *voracious*, which means *"always hungry for more."* One synonym for greed is covetousness. The rich young ruler was supposed to follow the commandments as a Jewish leader and a Pharisee.

The tenth commandment states:

"Neither shall thou desire thy neighbor's wife; neither shall thou covet thy neighbor's house, his field, his manservant, his maidservant, his ox, his ass, or anything that is thy neighbor's."

This young man had an insatiable appetite for money. Greed filled the rich young ruler. When greed enters our spirit, we rationalize our sins and justify our behavior. As if to say, "This is my wealth; why should I give it away?" One will rationalize and explain why their sinful mindset is okay. Someone may feel too far gone to be set free from such devastating perspectives. You can never be too far gone to be set free. The way out, as mentioned before, is the Four Step Release Method.

The entire process of this method gives you victory. However, there is a specific part of the process where greed is overcome. That is repentance or changing your mind about the sin that entangles you. You must realign your mind to seek and follow the supremacy of God in your heart. You must adjust your thinking and know that benevolence begins in the heart. The opposite of greed is contentment, and 1 Timothy 6:6-9 ensures that - *"Godliness with contentment is great gain. For we brought nothing into the world, and we can take nothing out of it. But if we have food and clothing, we will be content with that. Those who want to get rich fall into temptation and a trap and into many foolish and harmful desires that plunge people into ruin and destruction."* Being content with where you are and what you have will ease the wrongful desire of always wanting more.

Living a life of gratitude and contentment is a sure way to alleviate the effects of greed. However, this is not the only and best way. Delving into a deeper relationship and covenant with God will put you in the right standing with Him. The way to do that is to embrace the Four-Step Release Method. As you follow this Four-Step Release Method, you CAN and WILL obtain freedom from wherever you are in the progressive nature of sin by following these steps:

- Surrender
- Repentance
- Confession
- Crying out to God

Chapter 4: Greed

Questions to Consider

1. What happens once a person compromises and enters into rationalizing and justifying?

2. Why is it challenging, at this stage, to change the behavior associated with greed in the progressive nature of sin?

3. What is greed?

4. How does greed affect other stages in the progressive nature of sin?

5. How does the Four-Step Release Method contribute to alleviating greed?

Chapter 4: Greed
Questions to Consider

6. Where did the spirit of greed originate?

____

____

____

7. Why does God hate greed?

____

____

____

8. What does greed look like?

____

____

____

9. What was the first step of greed David had in 2 Samuel 11:1-9?

____

____

____

10. What is the first step to personal revival?

____

____

____

Chapter 4: Greed

Questions to Consider

11. What does the scripture in Proverbs 15:27 mean?

____

____

____

12. How else can greed be defined?

____

____

____

13. What issue has Jesus discussed most in the Bible besides the Kingdom of God?

____

____

____

14. Greed not only blinds you, but it also does what?

____

____

____

15. Where does the word greed come from?

____

____

____

Chapter 4: Greed
Questions to Consider

16. What is one synonym for greed?

17. What was the rich young ruler filled with, and why?

18. What will greed cause one to do?

19. Why is the tenth commandment an essential topic when discussing greed?

20. What does it mean to live a lifestyle of greed?

NOTES

NOTES

CHAPTER 5
Obsession

Discussion: How can obsession be hidden in the lives of believers?

When someone mentions the young ruler, I pray you will immediately think about all you have learned. We will exegesis this passage in Matthew 19:16-22 before concluding the last chapter in this book. I pray you will look at the progressive nature of sin in your lives and the lives of those around you. When you see a person whose life is marred by sin, you will not stand in the judgment seat of condemnation but with empathy, understanding, and compassion of how the enemy walked them up to the progressive nature of sin. I say this because your compassion for others will be their compassion for you when you fall.

How the Monkey is Caught

[16] *"And, behold, one came and said unto him, "Good Master, what good thing shall I do, that I may have eternal life?"* [17] *And he said unto him, "Why callest thou me good? There is non- good but one, God: But if thou wilt enters into life, keep the commandments."* [18] *He saith unto him, "Which ones?" Jesus said thou shalt not commit adultery, and Thou shalt not steal, Thou shalt not bear false witness,* [19] *Honor thy Father and thy mother: and, Thou shalt love thy neighbor as thyself.* [20] *The young man saith unto him, all these things have I kept from my*

youth up: What lack I yet? ²¹ Jesus said unto him, If thou wilt be perfect, go and sell that thou have and give to the poor, and thou shalt have treasure in heaven: and come and follow me. ²² But when the young man heard that saying, he went away sorrowful: for he had great possessions. Matthew 19:16-22

When we think about what could come after greed, it must be something that ultimately wreaks havoc on human existence. When we understand how greed has devastated our world and all its individuals, we see it as a hard act to follow. However, there is the fifth and final part of the progressive nature of sin: obsession. Obsession is the last part of the progressive nature of sin because when individuals become obsessed with something, they would rather have that object of their affection over the air to breathe. The monkey is caught becoming obsessed with the object.

When our sinful nature reaches the point of obsession, it becomes a place of total darkness. Somebody can call an obsessed person in our society a slacker; an obsessed person is an addict obsessed with the next drink, high, or fix. A person who is obsessed with someone is abusive. An obsessed person is a manipulator fixated on an object and will say or do anything to possess it. Someone obsessed with someone else's possession is a thief. An obsessed person is a rich young ruler so focused on acquiring wealth that he will sacrifice his salvation. An obsessed person is a person who has yielded themselves to the negative and darkest of dark forces of this world.

Furthermore, let's define this word. *Obsession* is a persistent disturbing preoccupation with an often-unreasonable idea or feeling. Obsession is to become so preoccupied with a sin that you forget that "God is the author and finisher of your faith." Obsession is the ultimate state of entrapment, where a person is spiritually whipped, physically beaten, morally depleted, and mentally tormented. Obsession is that place in your life where you are holding onto the banana, waiting for the hunter to come and capture your soul while still trying to rationalize yourself by walking away with the banana.

Examples of Biblical Obsession

There are a myriad of biblical examples of people who became obsessed. I want to share a couple with you and expand your understanding of the word obsessed. The Bible tells us that Pharaoh became obsessed with defying God's command. God sent ten plagues to let Pharaoh know He was a Sovereign God over everything, including Pharaoh, but Pharaoh still would not listen. Some might say, "Well, I am not obsessed like Pharaoh." I beg to differ. How many chances has God given you to turn from your wicked ways? How many plagues has He delivered you from in your life? How many people like Moses has He sent to remind you He loves you? Pharaoh was obsessed with control and a spirit of defiance.

This one is for the backsliders or those who have heard the word but chose not to live it. Saul, the king of the greatest nation on earth, is now considered a backslider. The Bible tells us that Saul was obsessed with his desire to kill David and keep his throne. Saul chased David because he wanted to keep his robe, crown, and kingdom, but what he lost was more significant than his robe, crown, or kingdom. He lost the relationship he had with God.

The Bible tells us:

"What good is it to gain the world and forfeit your soul" (NIV, 2011, Mark 8:36)?

Some folks who had a great relationship with God are reading this. Saul was obsessed with loss and battled the obsessions of fear, worry, and doubt. Like Saul, the things of this world got in your way.

"God has not given me the spirit of fear, but of power, love, and a sound mind" (NKJV, 1982, 2 Timothy 1:7).

And for my last one, the Bible tells us that King Herod was obsessed with keeping his kingdom. It was so much so that when he heard another King was born, he ordered all the first-born males to be killed. Babies were slaughtered in the streets because of Herod's obsession. King Herod was obsessed with stuff: recognition, power, position, status, and jealousy. Obsession devastated the lives of these three men, and obsession continues to ruin our lives today.

A World Filled with Obsession

We live in a world filled with obsessions. Our children or obsessed with games, technology, television, and everything else they can occupy their minds with except Jesus. Husbands are obsessed with their wives, and wives are obsessed with their husbands. Parents are obsessed with their children, forgetting Job's words, *"The Lord giveth, and the Lord taketh away; blesseth be the name of the Lord." Job 1:21.* We see the spirit of obsession everywhere we look. This last word paints a grim picture of all humanity. This last word paints a picture of hopelessness and despair.

Some Christians are so obsessed that they take lies for truths, wrongs for right, and falsehoods for facts. For example, those who are obsessed are in very abnormal conditions. Being obsessed is speaking something false and then thinking that one is correct. In the beginning, these Christians lie to deceive others. But in the end, they deceive themselves. When one lies, he deceives multiple people. He becomes habitual in lying and lies so much that he becomes convinced that he is speaking the truth. He becomes obsessed. When a man profoundly falls into self-deception, he believes everything is accurate. He could not tell what part was real or fake at a certain point. This type of self-deception is an obsession.

There is another kind of obsession. Some Christians seek and are desirous of going on appropriately before the Lord. Yet they do not have any light. Something may not be wrong, yet they think that they have done wrong and constantly worry about it if they say the Lord will no longer forgive them and the blood will no longer cleanse them. In God's eyes, they have not sinned. Yet they are very sure that they have sinned. They think they have done an irreparable wrong and committed an unforgivable sin. They are full of sorrow, and they weep. Assuming that one confession is not enough, they confess ten times or even a hundred times. Even while they acknowledge continuously, they feel their sin is still present. What is this? This is an obsession. One can be obsessed with more than just bad things. It is even possible to be obsessed with the sense of sin. If a seeking Christian does not have the light, he will condemn what he has not committed. This is an obsession. Being obsessed is believing something is real when it is not.

Isaiah 5:20 says, *"Woe to those who call good evil, and evil good; Who makes darkness light, And light darkness; Who makes bitterness sweetness, and sweetness bitterness!"*

A man can be so obsessed that he calls good evil and evil good; makes darkness light, and light darkness; makes bitterness sweetness and sweetness bitterness. He can be wrong and still be very confident that he is right. This is very pitiful. The worst thing that can happen to a Christian is to have sinned and be ignorant of it. To have sinned is a matter of blasphemy, but to be unaware of sin is a matter of darkness. Defilement is dangerous enough, but the danger is even greater if it is complemented by darkness. If a

Christian lives in darkness, it will not be easy to go on because he does not see.

A Christian can be obsessed with his thoughts, others' thoughts, his own words, others' words, his spiritual condition, his sins, or anything he has. Obsession is also a ubiquitous thing, and it can happen to any Christian. It can also be defined as doing something wrong and believing in your heart that it is the right thing. Being proud, stubborn, subjective, and confident, where even your conscience seems to justify your actions, this is an obsession. Obsession starts with imagination, with some subjective thoughts, with some strange belief from the unrenewed mind — and you think about these things, you mull them over until you get to where if you think about something long enough you believe it is real.

There are many symptoms of obsession. Of course, some are obsessed to a minor degree, others are obsessed to a greater degree, and some are obsessed to a severe degree. Ultimately, obsession is rooted in a stronghold. This stronghold can be areas of life, in mind, in people, where the enemy has a firm foothold, and he will not give it up easily. Therefore, we must pay attention to this matter.

The Story of John Newton

Despite our shortcomings, I want to end this book on a high note of hope and grace. In closing, I want to share a story about a man named John Newton. John Newton grew up in England. His Father was a sea captain, so he spent lots of time sailing.

As a young man, power lured him; he was tempted by money, compromised his moral standing with his heavenly Father, and greed prevented him from seeing the ills of his actions. The immoral and deplorable state in which he subjected his being for the sake of gain, ultimately, obsession, blinded him. It helped him justify and rationalize his twisted reasoning for buying and selling human lives.

The story of John Newton parallels the rich young ruler in that they had similar paths and gained wealth. One day, God prepared a storm at sea for this young man. This young man who had made his riches to be his god prayed to the God of the universe. His money could not save him. His position could not save him. Not even his skills could save him, but a loving and just God looked down on him with mercy and grace. God touched the boat amidst the storm, and John and all his cargo survived.

It did not happen immediately, but eventually, this young man became an Anglican priest who wrote 250 songs. One of them was called *Amazing Grace*.

As I conclude this topic, ask yourself these questions:

Is there hope for the obsessed? *Yes.*

Is there hope for the person lost in greed? *Yes.*

Is there hope for the person who compromises their moral standings with God? *Yes.*

Is there hope for the person who succumbs to temptation? *Yes.*

Is there hope for the person chasing after the lures? *Yes.*

Is there hope for the person who is right now, "Out of the will of God?" *Yes.*

Today, I have a confession. I am obsessed with going to heaven; I am obsessed with developing a relationship with Jesus; I am obsessed with living what I preach.

What is your obsession? Is it with the world or with Jesus? As you ponder and reflect on these questions, you know there is a way out of the vicious cycle of the progressive nature of sin. The way out is the Four-Step Release Method.

As mentioned before, you will get freedom from wherever you are in the progressive nature of sin by following these steps:

1. Surrender
2. Repentance
3. Confession
4. Crying out to God

Doing these things will be increasingly difficult based on what stage of the progressive nature of sin you are in. Surrender, repentance, and confession become more challenging as we rationalize and justify our behavior by the time we reach the obsession stage. However, all is not lost. You can find solace in knowing that God hears you, no matter where you are. You can be free from sin.

Chapter 5: Obsession
Questions to Consider

1. What happens to our sinful nature when it reaches the point of
    obsession?

    ____

    ____

    ____

2. What type of person is an obsessed person?

    ____

    ____

    ____

3. What is the definition of obsession?

    ____

    ____

    ____

4. Why is obsession the ultimate state of entrapment?

    ____

    ____

    ____

5. What did Pharaoh become obsessed with?

    ____

    ____

    ____

Chapter 5: Obsession

Questions to Consider

6. What was Saul obsessed with?

____

____

____

7. Why did Saul chase David?

____

____

____

8. What was King Herod's obsession?

____

____

____

9. How does the story of John Newton parallel the rich young ruler?

____

____

____

10. What are you obsessed with?

____

____

____

Chapter 5: Obsession
Questions to Consider

11. What is obsession rooted in?

____

____

____

12. What can a Christian be obsessed with?

____

____

____

13. What is the stronghold that obsession is rooted in?

____

____

____

14. In the story of John Newton, how did John survive?

____

____

____

15. How are addictive behavior and obsession closely related?

____

____

____

Chapter 5: Obsession

Questions to Consider

16. What does it mean to be obsessed with God?

____

____

____

17. How can Christians become obsessed and operate in deception?

____

____

____

18. How else can obsession be defined?

____

____

____

19. What does an obsessed person believe?

____

____

____

20. Where does obsession start?

____

____

____

NOTES

NOTES

Final Words

This book shows the reader how a primate is captured in the jungle. I also denote how a homo sapien is caught in a civilized environment. In all its infinite smartness, the monkey continues to hold on to the object at the bottom of the log, risking its capture and those in its group. The question I pose in this story is, "What would pose this knowledgeable animal to make such a terrible decision risking danger if not death? How can a man in infinite wisdom make the same mistake as a lesser species so undeveloped and unrefined? Now this question parallels the intelligence of man who has built skyscrapers reaching the depths of heaven, bridges crossing over the unimaginable, and bombs capable of destroying the world.

In this story, the parallel is also between the rich young ruler who seemed to have had everything but the one thing he had concluded only Jesus could offer him: eternal life.

Chapter 1 opens with the journey into the progressive nature of sin, looking at the first of the enemy's five steps to entrap a person's mind, body, and spirit. The word LURE is presented to the reader with grave details to leave nothing for the imagination so when one walks away from this experience, and they will truly understand the depth of this first step and how its entrapment captures the soul of a person.

TEMPTATION is the next word covering the second principle of the five-step process of the progressive nature of sin. There are many ways to define this word or break it down, but I will leave that up to the terms used in the story. But you need to know that our entrapment into sin does not come because the enemy is haphazard in his efforts to capture our souls. Temptation is nothing more than unconfessed lust or ill feeling waiting for exposure. So, in this next chapter, what is brought out about temptation helps the reader understand just how calculating the enemy is when it comes to his diabolical schemes created for the spiraling downfall of humanity.

In the third principle, I explain that the farther one goes into the progressive nature, the more difficult it becomes to separate oneself from the grips of sin. The third principle is COMPROMISE. The accomplice to the progressive nature of sin is JUSTIFICATION and RATIONALIZATION. Tying these words together is critical to explaining and understanding the model presented in this book.

From here, we move to the fourth word, GREED. The complexity of this word takes on many dimensions in the progressive nature of sin. Here king David becomes a poster boy for an in-depth understanding of this word and its complexities.

And finally, we end up at the final word on the progressive sin nature list, which is OBSESSION. This last word introduces the intensity of the sinful nature, highlighting the devastation of allowing the first four to culminate with this last word. King David is used again to show what happens when a person becomes obsessed with an object or person. This example brings the point home with clarity as to what happens when we fail to use the four-step release process to free ourselves from the progressive nature of the sin model. In this final stage, the emphasis is on entrapment and hopelessness.

Having said this, I would be remiss if I did not end with what I call the four-step release process. In each step of the progressive nature of sin, the escape clause is the release process. I mention in the book that one can call this personal process revival. The four-step release process is the way out, and I encourage anyone with their hand caught in the log to take full advantage of the release process.

Surrender, Repentance, Confession, and Crying out to God: These words are crucial in the life of all believers who choose to climb out of the progressive nature of sin.

About the Author

R ev. Dr. Tahlib McMicheaux is a highly driven change agent who was born to break barriers; he proves all things are possible when powered by purpose and faith in God.

From overcoming a learning disability that propelled him academically, earning his doctorate, to walking over 300 miles carrying a 60LB wooden cross to the State Capital in Sacramento, California, Rev. Dr. Tahlib McMicheaux is a living testimony of his motto, "Change your perspective, Change your outcome."

He has built his storied life and career brick by brick, fighting fears, failures, and setbacks to have the success he's always known was his to claim as a child of God. Yet, his greatest success is being a father to his three children and grandfather to his five grandbabies, who lovingly call him "Papa."

Having spent over 30 years in ministry, academia, and the mental health field as a community activist, thought leader, Dean of a Christian University, global speaker, and life coach, his work is a testament to what it means to leave an undeniable mark on the world.

Today, his projects include screenwriting, a second volume of his children's book *Daddy's Little Guls*, building a school in Rwanda, and getting people excited about the Word of God. He personifies what it means to ascend above adversity while inspiring countless others to do the same because he does not simply change lives — he expands them.

Rev. Dr. Tahlib McMicheaux can be contacted via email:

Email: BTLifeCoaching@gmail.com
Website: www.drtahlib.com
Instagram: @drtahlib

Answers to Chapter Questions

Chapter 1: Lure

1. **Q:** What is the purpose of a *Lure*?

   A: The stealth of the lure lies in its ability to mimic the movements of what one craves above all else. It grabs your attention, intending to draw you toward temptation.

2. **Q:** How many meanings does the noun *Lure* have? What are they?

   A: There are three (3) meanings for the noun *Lure.*
   They are:
   • Qualities that attract by seeming to promise some reward (physical, spiritual, or emotional);
   • Anything that serves as an enticement;
   • Something used to coerce victims into danger.

3. **Q:** What is temptation luring you away from?

   A: Your Savior

4. **Q:** What is temptation luring you to?

   A: To Hell

5. **Q:** Why is the power of lust underestimated?

   A: *Answers can vary.* Satan **knows** you better than you know yourself. He has been studying you as he did when he observed Job before attacking him. He knows your weaknesses and your lures. Lust leads to *Lures.*

6. **Q:** Why did Jesus offer the rich young ruler an invitation to have fellowship with him?

    A: *Answers can vary.* Jesus held him in high esteem.

7. **Q:** What is the first word representing the progressive nature of sin?

    A: *Lure*

8. **Q:** How does a lure attract you?

    A: A lure will attract you by fulfilling a need you didn't even know you had.

9. **Q:** Why does the enemy study your weakness?

    A: *Answers can vary.* Satan will start working on creating the so-called perfect, comfortable situation to feed into your lures and lusts, ultimately catching you off guard.

10. **Q:** Why is it important to confess your sins?

    A: Have a clear conscience and remove barriers between you and God.

11. **Q:** What book of the Bible uses lure as a description for a woman? What is her name?

    A: The book of the Bible that uses lure as a description for a woman in Proverbs. Her name is Folly.

12. **Q:** What are the various lures?

    A: Curiosity, insecurity, power, pride, ego, clout, position, and self-sufficiency

13. **Q:** What is a sinful nature?

    A: The sinful nature is that nature in man that makes him rebellious against God.

14. **Q**: What were the Rich Young Ruler's lures?

    A: *Answers can vary.* His lure could have been power, clout, status, and want to appear more important than he was.

15. **Q**: What are two powerful lures that have captured more humans who act like the monkey in the story?

    A: Curiosity and Insecurity

16. **Q**: How can you protect yourself from the progressive nature of sin?

    A: *Answers can vary.* *"And do not be conformed to this world, but be transformed by the renewing of your mind, that you may prove what is that good and acceptable and perfect will of God" (NKJV, 1982, Romans 12:2). But seek first the kingdom of God and His righteousness, and all these things shall be added to you"(NKJV, 1982, Matthew 6:33). "For the wages (cost of being steeped in something) of sin is death, but the gift of God is eternal life in Christ Jesus our Lord" (NKJV, 1982, Romans 6:23).*

17. **Q**: What made the rich young ruler compromise his external existence for his earthly wealth?

    A: Rationalization and Justifying

18. **Q**: What are the definitions of rationalizing and justifying?

    A: Rationalizing — attempting to explain or justify behavior or an attitude for logical reasons, even if these are inappropriate. Justifying — showing or proving to be reasonable.

19. **Q**: What is the only way you can be transformed?

    A: Through the personal revival

20. **Q**: What is the Four Step Release Method?

    A: Surrender, repentance, confession, and crying out to God

Chapter 2: Temptation

1. **Q**: What kept the rich young ruler from reaching his desired goal?

   A: He held onto worldly possessions.

2. **Q**: What is the definition of the word temptation?

   A: Temptation is the desire to do something wrong or unwise.

3. **Q**: Who is a person who continues to experience God but is never transformed by God?

   A: An undisciplined believer

4. **Q**: What stops a person from being transformed by God?

   A: Doubt and lack of faith do not allow them to commit themselves to the process that reaps true transformation.

5. **Q**: What makes you an easy target for the enemy?

   A: When you are undisciplined, you become an easy target for the enemy.

6. **Q**: How do I fight temptation?

   A: You have got to plant yourself in the Word of God to resist the enemy. You have got to put on the whole armor of God. You have got to crucify the old nature daily, and you have got to allow your mind to be transformed.

7. **Q**: When have you progressed from sinning to being a sinner?

   A: When you get to this place, you are holding onto the banana, thinking that nobody knows you have progressed from sin to becoming a sinner. You walk around with a banana in your hands as if no one is looking at it.

8. **Q:** Is God tempting me?

   A: God cannot be tempted, nor does He tempt anyone, so the temptation is not of God.

9. **Q:** How do I praise God for trials in my life when I go through them?

   A: To praise God for the trials in your life, you need to know the difference between a trial and a temptation.

10. **Q:** Why is God so particular about trusting us with the Word? Why does God have to trust us with His Word?

    A: When you seek God through His Word, He will reveal Himself in His Word. When you seek God through His Word, He will reveal Himself in His Word. Essentially, He is trusting you with Himself and His secrets.

11. **Q:** What is an example of a trial?

    A: A righteous man named Job went from riches to poverty. He went from popularity to disdain. His family was taken from him, and his faithful wife abandoned him in his time of need. Job's friends came to console him and wound-up judging and condemning him. He lost everything but was given back double because he endured the test.

12. **Q:** What is the purpose of temptation and trials?

    A: Temptation comes to bring us down, but the trials take us to another level of consciousness.

13. **Q:** What will a trial do in your life?

    A: The trial will take you to the edge, but it will not take you over. If you go over, it is probably not a trial. 1 Corinthian 10:3 tells us that God will not put any more on us than we can handle.

14. **Q:** What is the guaranteed outcome of going through a trial?

    A: God will get the glory, and you will get the victory from your trial.

15. **Q:** When enduring a trial, can Satan bring temptation into my life?

    A: Yes, the temptation is there to move you away from your trial so that you will not be proven genuine and trustworthy.

16. **Q:** What do we know about trials?

    A: God will not leave me are forsake me when I am in a trial or ever; Your trials will not last forever; Your trials are an opportunity to show God that you are genuine and trustworthy; When God brings me out, He will get the glory for my victory.

17. **Q:** From where do these temptations come?

    A: First, they do not come from God, although He allows them. James 1:13 says, "For God cannot be tempted by evil, and He does not tempt anyone." According to the passage, temptations come from Satan.

18. **Q:** How do we resist temptations?

    A: All our efforts to resist will be ineffective unless they are powered by the Holy Spirit through constant reading, studying, and meditating on the Word.

19. **Q:** How are we drawn into sin?

    A: We are drawn through our imagination, desires, physical pleasure, spiritual power, and emotional dominance.

20. **Q:** What are addictions?

    A: Addictions are nothing more than repeated behaviors we succumb to and make excuses for.

Chapter 3: Compromise

1. **Q:** What is compromise?

   A: It is a settlement of differences in which each side makes a concession.

2. **Q:** Why do compromising believers prefer to be around compromising people?

   A: Because uncompromising people will hold them accountable for living up to a higher standard.

3. **Q:** Why would God allow you to go through life thinking that you have fooled everyone around you, only to discover you had not deceived Him?

   A: *'"Not everyone who says to me, 'Lord, Lord,' will enter the kingdom of heaven, but only the one who does the will of My Father who is in heaven. Many will say to me on that day, 'Lord, Lord, did we not prophesy in your name and your name drive out demons and, in your name, perform many miracles?'" Then I will tell them plainly, "'I never knew you. Away from me, you evildoers'"* (NIV, 2011, Matthew 7:21–23)!

4. **Q:** Do you want to know what God thinks about your decision to compromise with the enemy?

   A: You are unstable in all your ways. *"A double-minded man is unstable in all his ways,"* James 1:8.

5. **Q:** What is the first phase of the internal demise of our will to resist the enemy?

   A: Compromising is the first phase of the internal demise of our will to resist the enemy.

6. **Q:** Who lived by the Oral Law?

   A: The Pharisees

7. **Q:** How can the adversary's influence be resisted and overcome?

   A: By using the power and tools that God has given us.

8. **Q:** How do we resist the devil?

   A: We resist the devil by being ruled by the inerrant Word of God and taking precautions not to grieve the Holy Spirit.

9. **Q:** What are the warning signs of compromise, and how can we respond appropriately?

   A: One significant sign of compromise is changing the Word of God to fit with the changing world.

10. **Q:** Why didn't the Rich Young Ruler give up his wealth for eternal life if he believed in eternal life, the Ten Commandments, and the Messiah?

    A: Somewhere in his life, he had been lured to temptation and grabbed onto the world's desires while being tempted. His mind became filled with justifying and rationalizing why he should hold on to the banana in his hand, even if it cost him his eternal life.

11. **Q:** What is a way that you can be transformed?

    A: You can be transformed by the renewing of your mind.

12. **Q:** When you find a compromising person, you will most likely find what?

    A: You will find someone astute at rationalizing and justifying things to work out in their favor.

13. **Q:** Who was the rich young ruler?

    A: A Jewish leader who had administrative authority and great wealth.

14. **Q:** What did the Pharisees believe?

    A: They believed that the Law God gave Moses was twofold: the Written Law and the Oral Law, i.e., the prophets' teachings and the Jewish people's oral traditions.

15. **Q:** Can a person compromise even if they have a firm understanding of the Word of God?

    A: Yes. All it takes is for that person to give the lure in their life's attention, leading to temptation and then compromise.

16. **Q:** Why do some progressing Christians live lives that are not keeping with the precepts of the scripture?

    A: For them, the things of the world and its sensual allurements take precedence over the Word of God.

17. **Q:** What does Jesus refer to these people as?

    A: *"Those who hear the word, but the care of the world and the deceitfulness of riches and the desires for other things, enter and choke the word, and it proves unfruitful"* (NKJV, 1982, Matthew 13:22).

18. **Q:** What makes a person an uncompromising believer?

    A: A person is an uncompromising believer when they do not succumb to the lust of their flesh.

19. **Q:** What does compromising your walk with God do to your spiritual life?

A: Compromising your walk with God hinders you and confuses others seeking to follow Christ.

20. **Q:** What is the Four Step Release Method?

A: The Four Step Release Method: Surrender, Repentance, Confession, and Crying out to God.

Chapter 4: Greed

1. **Q:** What happens once a person compromises and enters rationalizing and justifying?

   A: Greed becomes an overpowering behavior that causes a person to think, act, and behave unreasonably.

2. **Q:** Why is it challenging to change this behavior into the progressive nature of sin at this point?

   A: It is challenging to change this behavior into the progressive nature of sin because greed is overpowering, and it is difficult to overcome it alone.

3. **Q:** What is greed?

   A: Greed is an overwhelming urge to have more of something, usually more than what you need.

4. **Q:** Where does greed come from?

   A: It comes from always wanting more, whether it is money, clothes, television, food, drink, or anything else we consume or purchase in excess.

5. **Q:** From where did the spirit of greed come?

   A: Satan's jealousy in heaven turned into greed because he could not get enough power.

6. **Q:** Where did the spirit of greed originate?

   A: The spirit of greed is the same one that got kicked out of heaven. It is now running rampant throughout the earth.

7. **Q:** Why does God hate greed?

   A: God hates greed because it is devoid of empathy and compassion.

8. **Q:** What does greed look like?

   A: When you see greed, it is an ugly spirit that causes the soul of humankind to become contorted, seeking only to please self.

9. **Q:** What was the first step of greed David had in 2 Samuel 11:1-9?

   A: David justifies, rationalizes, and attempts to cover up his sins. David had fallen out of personal revival by operating in unadulterated evil.

10. **Q:** What is the first step to personal revival?

    A: The first step in personal revival is to own your sins before God.

11. **Q:** What does the scripture in Proverbs 15:27 mean?

    A: The desire to be rich is dangerous to a man's family. He will be tempted to accept bribes or compromise righteousness, bringing trouble to his wife, children, and estate. But a man that hates bribes or financial compromise will preserve and prosper his family.

12. **Q:** How else can greed be defined?

    A: Greed is the defining characteristic of human nature and the desire to own or control more resources than others.

13. **Q:** What issue has Jesus discussed most in the Bible besides the Kingdom of God?

    A: Money and Greed

14. **Q:** Greed not only blinds you, but it does what?

    A: It hardens your heart, causing you to hold on to the banana, justifying why you cannot let go.

15. **Q:** Where does the word greed come from?

    A: From the Old English *grædig*, or *voracious*, which means "always hungry for more."

16. **Q:** What is one synonym for greed?

    A: Covetousness

17. **Q:** What was the rich young ruler filled with, and why?

    A: He was filled with greed because he had an insatiable appetite for money.

18. **Q:** What will greed cause one to do?

    A: One will rationalize and explain why their sinful mindset is okay.

19. **Q:** Why is the 10th commandment essential to discuss when discussing greed?

    A: It is important to discuss because "neither shall thou desire thy neighbor's wife; neither shall thou covet thy neighbor's house, his field, his manservant, his maidservant, his ox, his ass, or anything that is thy neighbor's." We are to avoid coveting anything that does not belong to us.

20. **Q:** Do you agree that greed is a deadly sin? Why?

    A: Answers will vary.

Chapter 5: Obsession

1. **Q:** What happens to our sinful nature when it reaches the point of obsession?

    A: It becomes a place of total darkness.

2. **Q**: What type of person is an obsessed person?

    A: An abusive person

3. **Q**: What is the definition of obsession?

    A: Obsession is a persistent disturbing preoccupation with an often-unreasonable idea or feeling.

4. **Q:** Why is obsession the ultimate state of entrapment?

    A: Obsession is the ultimate state of entrapment because a person is spiritually whipped, physically beaten, morally depleted, and mentally tormented. Obsession is that place in your life where you are holding onto the banana, waiting for the hunter to come and capture your soul while still trying to rationalize yourself by walking away with the banana.

5. **Q**: What did Pharaoh become obsessed with?

    A: Pharaoh became obsessed with defying God's command.

6. **Q**: What was Saul obsessed with?

    A: Saul was obsessed with his desire to kill David and keep his throne.

7. **Q**: Why did Saul chase David?

    A: Saul chased David because he wanted to keep his robe, crown, and kingdom.

8. **Q:** What was King Herod's obsession?

   A: King Herod was obsessed with stuff: recognition, power, position, status, and jealousy.

9. **Q**: How does the story of John Newton parallel the rich young ruler?

   A: The story of John Newton parallels the rich young ruler in that they had similar paths and gained wealth.

10. **Q:** What are you obsessed with?

    A: **Answers will vary.**

11. **Q**: What is obsession rooted in?

    A: A stronghold. This stronghold can be areas of life, in mind, in people, where the enemy has a firm foothold, and he will not give it up easily.

12. **Q**: What can a Christian be obsessed with?

    A: A Christian can be obsessed with his thoughts, others' thoughts, his own words, others' words, his spiritual condition, his sins, or anything he has.

13. **Q**: What is the stronghold that obsession is rooted in?

    A: This stronghold can be areas of life, in mind, in people, where the enemy has a firm foothold, and he will not give it up easily.

14. **Q**: In the story of John Newton, how did John survive?

    A: God touched the boat amidst the storm.

15. **Q**: How is addictive behavior and obsession closely related?

    A: When you are addicted to something, it becomes a habit that becomes an obsession. You are a prisoner locked up by deception.

16. **Q:** What does it mean to be obsessed with God?

    A: To be obsessed with God is to have an effective barricade against all the assaults of the enemy.

17. **Q:** How can Christians become obsessed and operate in deception?

    A: Christians can become obsessed by thinking of something we want so much that eventually it becomes normal for us — even when we are presented with the truth concerning that obsession.

18. **Q:** How else can obsession be defined?

    A: To be obsessed is to do the wrong thing and believe in your heart that it is the right thing. Being proud, stubborn, subjective, and confident, where even your conscience seems to justify your actions as an obsession.

19. **Q:** What does an obsessed person believe?

    A: An obsessed person believes falsehood to be truth and firmly upholds his falsehood to be the absolute truth.

20. **Q:** Where does obsession start?

    A: Obsession starts with imagination, with some subjective thoughts, with some strange belief from the unrenewed mind — and you think about these things, you mull over them until you get to where you think something long enough that you believe it has become real.

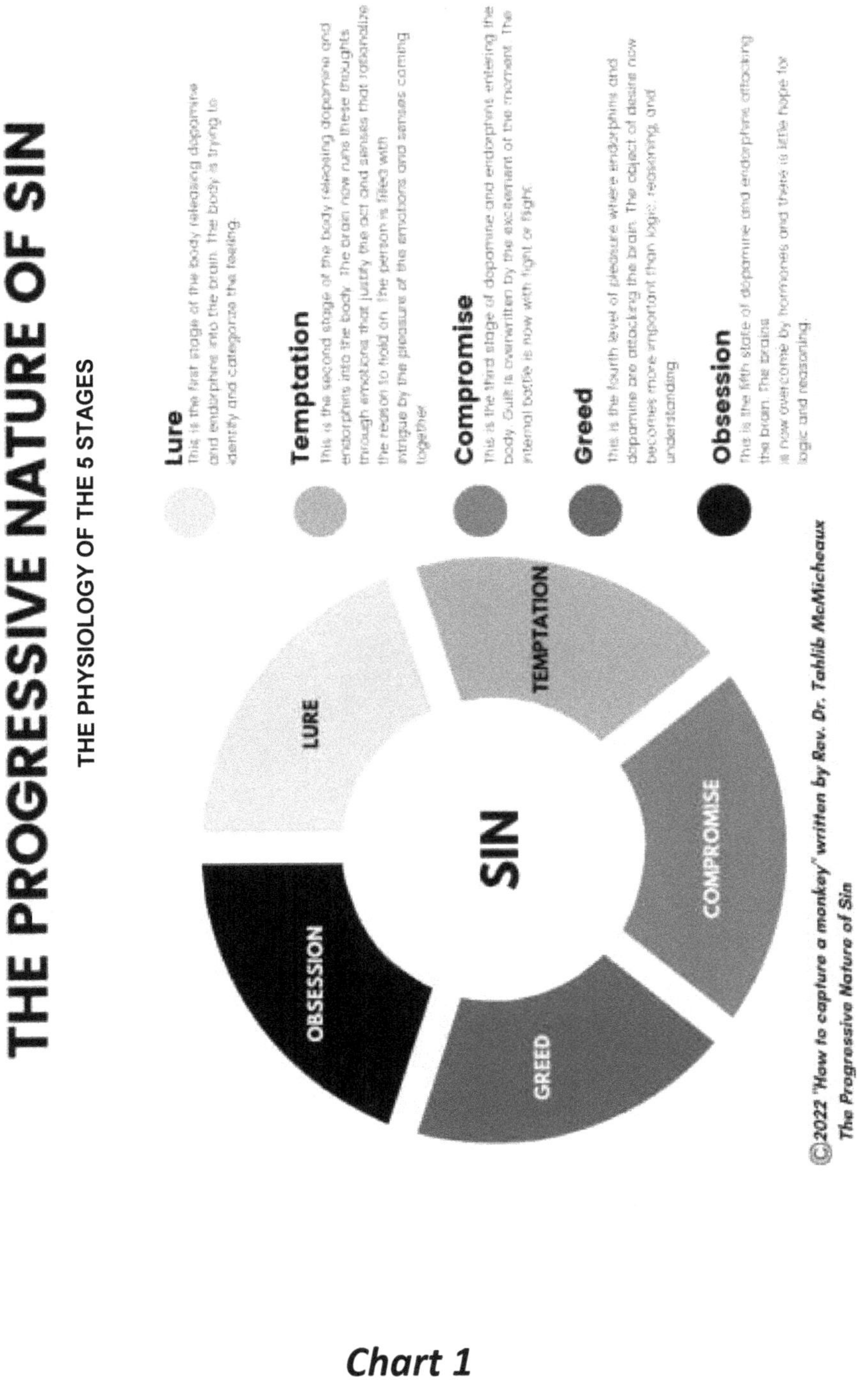
THE PROGRESSIVE NATURE OF SIN
THE PHYSIOLOGY OF THE 5 STAGES
OBSESSION
LURE
SIN
GREED
TEMPTATION
COMPROMISE
Lure
This is the first stage of the body releasing dopamine and endorphins into the brain. The body is trying to identify and categorize the feeling.
Temptation
This is the second stage of the body releasing dopamine and endorphins into the body. The brain now runs these thoughts through emotions that justify the act and senses that rationalize the reason to hold on. The person is filled with intrigue by the pleasure of the emotions and senses coming together.
Compromise
This is the third stage of dopamine and endorphins entering the body. Guilt is overwritten by the excitement of the moment. The internal battle is now with fight or flight.
Greed
This is the fourth level of pleasure where endorphins and dopamine are attacking the brain. The object of desire now becomes more important than logic, reasoning, and understanding.
Obsession
This is the fifth state of dopamine and endorphins attacking the brain. The brains is now overcome by hormones and there is little hope for logic and reasoning.
©2022 "How to capture a monkey" written by Rev. Dr. Tahlib McMicheaux
The Progressive Nature of Sin

Chart 1

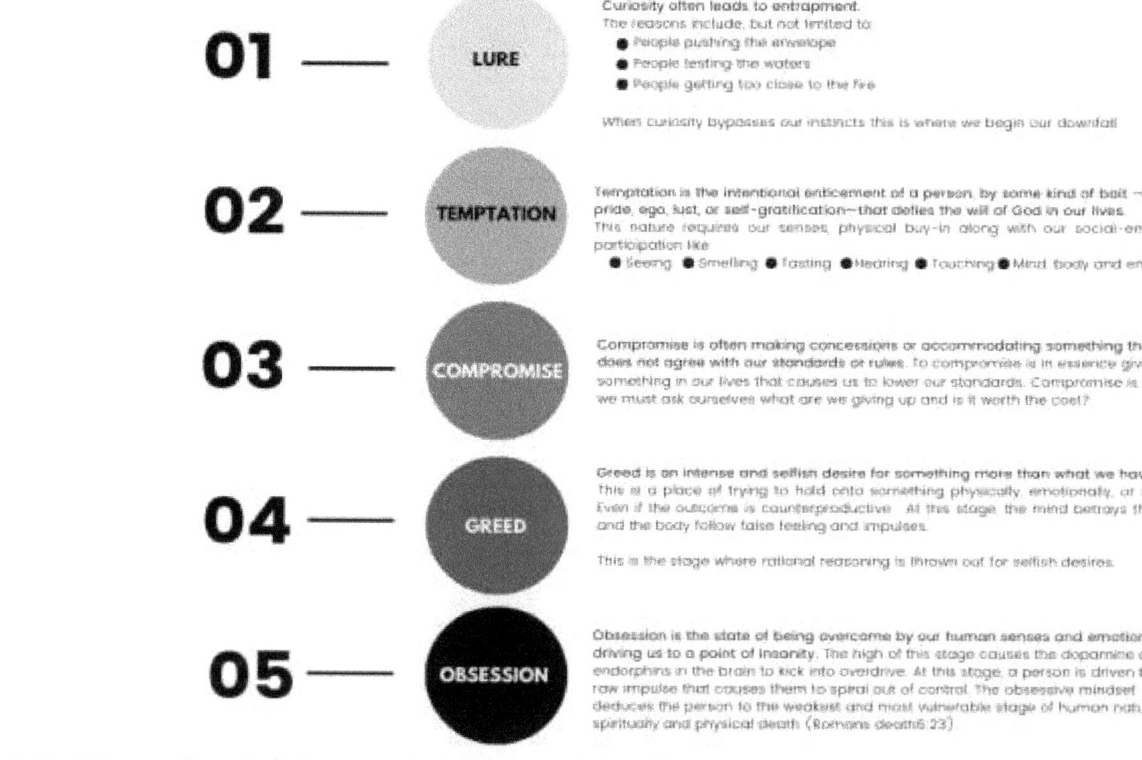

THE SPIRITUAL DECLINE OF THE 5 STAGES OF SIN
01 — LURE
Curiosity often leads to entrapment.
The reasons include, but not limited to:
● People pushing the envelope
● People testing the waters
● People getting too close to the fire
When curiosity bypasses our instincts this is where we begin our downfall.
02 — TEMPTATION
Temptation is the intentional enticement of a person, by some kind of bait —usually pride, ego, lust, or self-gratification—that defies the will of God in our lives. This nature requires our senses, physical buy-in along with our social-emotional participation like:
● Seeing ● Smelling ● Tasting ● Hearing ● Touching ● Mind, body and emotions
03 — COMPROMISE
Compromise is often making concessions or accommodating something that does not agree with our standards or rules. To compromise is in essence giving up something in our lives that causes us to lower our standards. Compromise is where we must ask ourselves what are we giving up and is it worth the cost?
04 — GREED
Greed is an intense and selfish desire for something more than what we have. This is a place of trying to hold onto something physically, emotionally, or socially. Even if the outcome is counterproductive. At this stage, the mind betrays the body and the body follow false feeling and impulses.
This is the stage where rational reasoning is thrown out for selfish desires.
05 — OBSESSION
Obsession is the state of being overcome by our human senses and emotions driving us to a point of insanity. The high of this stage causes the dopamine and endorphins in the brain to kick into overdrive. At this stage, a person is driven by the raw impulse that causes them to spiral out of control. The obsessive mindset deduces the person to the weakest and most vulnerable stage of human nature, spiritually and physical death (Romans deaths 23)